Sin Sick

Sin Sick

Moral Injury in War and Literature

Joshua Pederson

Cornell University Press

Ithaca and London

First published 2021 by Cornell University Press

Library of Congress Cataloging-in-Publication Data

Names: Pederson, Joshua, author.
Title: Sin sick : moral injury in war and literature / Joshua Pederson.
Description: Ithaca [New York] : Cornell University Press, 2021. |
    Includes bibliographical references and index.
Identifiers: LCCN 2020044049 (print) | LCCN 2020044050 (ebook) |
    ISBN 9781501755873 (hardcover) | ISBN 9781501755880 (epub) |
    ISBN 9781501755897 (pdf)
Subjects: LCSH: Psychic trauma in literature. | Moral conditions
    in literature. | War in literature.
Classification: LCC PN56.P914 P43 2021 (print) |
    LCC PN56.P914 (ebook) | DDC 809/.93581—dc23
LC record available at https://lccn.loc.gov/2020044049
LC ebook record available at https://lccn.loc.gov/2020044050

There is a balm in Gilead
To make the wounded whole
There is a balm in Gilead
To heal the sin-sick soul

—Traditional hymn

Contents

Acknowledgments

I owe gratitude to so many who offered help and encouragement as I worked through this book these last few years.

I'm especially grateful to my friend and mentor Shelly Rambo, whose work on trauma is a model for my own. She is an exemplary scholar, educator, and colleague, and I'm thankful for her gracious support and her excellent cocktail recommendations. Special thanks also to our coteacher, Ellen DeVoe, without whose keen insights (and admirable intellectual generosity) this book would be the weaker.

In a similar vein, Brett Litz and Jennifer Wortmann—both moral injury specialists—were generous enough to read multiple drafts of this book's early chapters. Any remaining defects are my own, but I am confident these passages are markedly stronger as a result of their fine suggestions. Thanks also to my undergraduate research assistants, Shelby Aguilar and Andrew Ippolito, who provided integral aid in constructing the Works Cited list.

I count myself lucky to have such a warm academic home at Boston University's College of General Studies. I thank Dean Natalie McKnight for maintaining such a welcoming community and for supporting all the teacher-scholars who work there, myself included. Thanks also to Adam Sweeting, both for guidance on this project and for rallying to my cause even after inheriting me from another chair; I am grateful for your kindness, your rectitude, and your always-open door. Regards also to my recent teammates, Sandra Buerger and Benjamin Varat; it's a pleasure and an honor to teach with you.

More thanks to the many friends who provided encouragement and company while the piece was coming together. To list them all would take another page, but I single out Ryan and Kelly Kurlbaum and John and Shannon Mackey, all of whom talked through the project with me repeatedly and at length. I aspire to be as good a friend to all as you are to me.

Finally, to my parents, Tom and Nancy; my brother and sister-in-law, Lukas and Cate; and my in-laws, David and Mary, I am infinitely fortunate to have landed in such a caring, attentive family. My love to you all. And to my wife, Jessica, and my kids, Judah and Rosalind: you are my home base and my shelter from the storm. I adore you.

Portions of this book previously appeared in "Moral Injury in Literature," *Narrative* 28.1 (2020): 43–61.

Sin Sick

Introduction

WHY WE NEED MORAL INJURY NOW

It is difficult to overstate the influence of trauma theory to the field of literary criticism over the past quarter century. When Cathy Caruth, Shoshana Felman, Geoffrey Hartman, and a handful of other theorists began writing about trauma and art in the middle of the 1990s, they laid the foundation for a promising new mode of criticism that continues to bear fruit to this day. Trauma theory represents one of the most productive brands of interdisciplinary literary study, smartly integrating the insights of psychology into our interpretation of text and image. It acts as a potent vindication of the power of art to bear witness to our deepest hurts. And it has spurred the development (or reinvigoration) of other important contemporary schools of criticism, notably affect theory and memory studies. Yet trauma theory has always had a blind spot: the psychic pain associated with wrongdoing. Though scholars occasionally discuss what is sometimes referred to as "perpetrator trauma," they often end up stumbling on the uncomfortable fact that while the pain of trauma resembles the pain of perpetration, the two are not identical.

This book is an attempt to rectify that shortcoming by introducing (or perhaps reintroducing) the idea of moral injury (MI) to literary studies. As this volume's title and epigraph suggest, moral injury is something like being "sin sick," in the words of the old hymn. Or in slightly different terms, MI is a novel concept that defines and describes the lingering negative effects that afflict those who do or witness wrong. Indeed, moral injury and its antecedents have a long if unacknowledged literary history, and in the pages that follow, I will begin tracing it. I also contend that moral injury shapes not only the substance but also the style of literature—that a number of tropes often cluster around it. Often if not always, accounts of moral injury in literature are accompanied by a dark excess, a looming evil that encroaches and threatens to spread. This excess manifests formally in a few distinct ways, each of which is anticipated by George Bataille in his writings on the theme.

Jason Wayne LeMieux is a Marine with three tours in Iraq. Since the end of his service, LeMieux has often argued that loosened rules of engagement during parts of that conflict put him and his fellow service members in situations where they were much more likely to kill civilians. As one example, he tells the story of a commander's decision during a bloody mission in Anbar to relax the rules of engagement so dramatically that the unit could effectively fire at anyone: "Later [my commander] ordered that *everyone* in the streets was an enemy combatant" (Iraq Veterans 18). The order had predictably catastrophic results. LeMieux continues:

> I can remember one instance that afternoon when we came around a corner and an unarmed Iraqi man stepped out of a doorway. I remember the marine directly in front of me raising his rifle and aiming at the unarmed man. . . . [T]he next thing I remember is stepping over the dead man's body to clear the room that he came out of. It was a storage room and it was full of some Arabic version of Cheetos. There weren't any weapons in the area except ours" (Iraq Veterans 18).

LeMieux notes that incidents like these caused real anguish for him and his fellow troops—especially those who served multiple tours. Though shooting a person who is not obviously a combatant under orders may feel necessary in the moment, it seldom does after, and the toll on our veterans is high. Any number can recount in excruciating detail the pain they still carry from killing in wartime. Yet according to Edward Tick—a psychoanalyst with nearly four decades of experience counseling veterans—most contemporary therapy models do a poor job helping service members grapple with this type of torment. He writes, "Veterans often complain, 'Our therapists will not talk to us about the killing we have done, but only what was done to us. They treat us like victims, but we have perpetrator PTSD'" (83). Clearly this problem is real, and there have been some efforts to address what Tick calls "perpetrator PTSD."[1] To this effect, Rachel MacNair has even proposed the development of a new subcategory of PTSD that she calls "perpetration-induced traumatic stress" (or PITS). Yet such neologisms grate. For isn't PTSD more frequently associated with victimization, not perpetration? Or, in blunter terms, we might imagine that a child who witnessed her parents' murder at My Lai would be "traumatized" by that experience, but would we want to say the same of the soldier who pulled the trigger? Indeed, problems arise when we try to discuss "perpetrator trauma" and apply trauma-theoretical insights to the suffering of those who do or witness bad acts.[2] Three stories demonstrate some of the shortcomings of the trauma model when it is applied to the anguish associated with wrongdoing.

In the early morning hours of February 14, 2013, the Olympian and Paralympic sprinting champion Oscar Pistorius fired multiple gunshots through the door of his own bathroom, killing his girlfriend, Reeva Steenkamp. Pistorius—nicknamed "Blade Runner" for the carbon-fiber prostheses on which he ran—claimed that he believed Steenkamp was an intruder and that he shot in self-defense. Prosecutors disagreed, and Pistorius went on trial for murder the following year in Pretoria. News of the trial blanketed South Africa's front pages through the summer of 2014, but many stories were dedicated to Pistorius's apparent anguish both on the stand and off. The athlete's psychological state was global news: the *New York Times* published nearly a dozen features that mentioned Pistorius's apparent torment. Throughout the proceedings, the defendant was visibly upset, often tearing up, sobbing, vomiting, praying, or swooning (Lyall). And a psychologist's report read aloud during the trial argued that he needed treatment for post-traumatic stress (Cowell). For his defense team, this purported trauma was evidence of his innocence; Berkeley law professor Saira Mohamed explained, "If he was haunted by her death, then surely he could not be the bad guy in this scenario: He was the aggrieved victim of a terrible loss, not the heartless killer of an innocent woman" (Mohamed 1173). Indeed, the judge's sympathy at his grief may have contributed to the lightness of Pistorius's initial sentence; she found him guilty of "culpable homicide" and gave him just ten months in prison. The prosecution quickly appealed and eventually secured a murder conviction in 2016, but even the new sentence was shorter than prosecutors recommended. In making him eligible for parole halfway through a six-year prison term, the judge cited "mitigating factors" like the defendant's remorse. But as Mohamed notes, neither Pistorius's remorse nor his anguish have anything to do with his guilt or innocence. His pain says "nothing about whether he murdered his girlfriend or lost her in a tragic accident. It tells us only that he now suffers" (1173). Yet when we look at Pistorius's suffering through the trauma lens, we are tempted—wrongly—both to see his crimes in a softer light and to forget the real victims of Blade Runner's violence: Steenkamp and her family.

Another story demonstrates how an overextension of the trauma model may allow us to avoid questions of not only personal but collective responsibility. Chris Kyle is often lauded as the greatest sniper in US military history. Through four tours in Iraq, he garnered more confirmed kills—160—than any other sniper. In an evaluation, Kyle's commanding officer wrote that his "performance under fire cannot be overstated," and because of his skill and valor, he was twice recommended to join Seal Team Six, the unit that would be responsible for the death of Osama bin Laden (Schmidle). However, when he was home, he was haunted by his time in country. Clint Eastwood focuses on Kyle's psychic pain in *American Sniper*, a film version of his life that demonstrates the "extremes of psychological torment our hero must endure" (Scranton, "Trauma"). And yet as the novelist and Iraq War veteran Roy Scranton argues, Eastwood's decision to direct our attention to Kyle's suffering and ask us to think narrowly about his "trauma" is troubling. Scranton writes,

> *American Sniper* focuses in tight on one man's story of trauma, leaving out the complex questions of why Kyle was in Iraq being traumatized in the first place. The Iraqis in the film are villains, caricatures, and targets, and the only real opinion on them the film offers is Kyle's. The Iraqis are all "savages" who threaten American lives and need to be killed. There's some truth in this representation, insofar as this is how a lot of American soldiers thought. Yet the film obviates the questions of why *any* American soldiers were in Iraq, why they stayed there for eight years, why they had to kill thousands upon thousands of Iraqi civilians, and how we are to understand the long and ongoing bloodbath once called the "war on terror." It does that precisely by turning a killer into a victim, a war hero into a trauma hero. ("Trauma")

To tell the soldier's story in terms of *his* pain is to avoid discussion of the exponentially greater pain his presence in Iraq inflicted on the family and friends of the scores of individuals he killed.[3] Further, to ignore these deaths is to avoid considering the ways they may have contributed to and colored Kyle's suffering. Finally, framing his biography in terms of his "trauma" also lets Eastwood avoid critical analysis of the Iraq War more broadly considered, and the likely hundreds of thousands of Iraqi lives that conflict brutally erased.[4] Certainly, one can acknowledge Kyle's suffering. But thinking of him as "traumatized" allows us to consider him first and foremost as a victim while at the same time ignoring the many victims of his violence.

Of course, "perpetrator PTSD" doesn't create problems only for clinicians and psychologists, judges and juries, service members and veterans. It has also tripped up literary critics. In the opening pages of her potent, field-defining work *Unclaimed Experience*, Cathy Caruth presents us with what she believes to be an instructive image of trauma in literature borrowed (via Freud) from the pages of Tasso's *Gerusalemme Liberata*. In that text, the hero Tancred unknowingly "kills his beloved Clorinda in a duel while she is disguised in the armour of an enemy knight. After her burial he makes his way into a strange magic forest. . . . He slashes with his sword at a tall tree; but blood streams from the cut and the voice of Clorinda, whose soul is imprisoned in the tree, is heard complaining that he has wounded his beloved once again" (quoted in Caruth, *Unclaimed* 2). The story is one of many examples Caruth provides in developing her influential model: Tancred's pain at the loss of his love is an exemplary trauma, and the image of the speaking wound attests to the fact that the voice of trauma "stubbornly persists in bearing witness" to our deepest hurts (Caruth, *Unclaimed* 3). Yet Caruth's use of Tancred has rubbed more than one critic the wrong way, for isn't it more accurate to think of him not as the one who suffers pain, but as the one who inflicts it? As Stef Craps puts it, "Caruth thus effectively rewrites the wound inflicted on Clorinda as a trauma suffered by Tancred" (15). In her zealous critique of Caruth in *Trauma: A Genealogy*, Ruth Leys enumerates problems that might arise from such a transposition. For Leys, this confusion has "chilling implications": "Caruth's logic would turn other perpetrators into victims too—for example, it would turn the executioners of the Jews into victims and the 'cries' of the Jews into testimony to the trauma suffered by the Nazis" (297).[5]

Leys overplays her hand here. For there is little in *Unclaimed Experience* to suggest that Caruth's model is intended to light the way to a mourning model for the Auschwitz commandant. Yet the kernel of Leys's argument stands, for it seems so obvious that Tancred's suffering must be qualitatively different from Clorinda's. And accepting—or arguing—that it is not is both logically and ethically problematic. Applying the trauma model to Pistorius *and* Steenkamp, Kyle *and* Iraqi civilians, or Tancred *and* Clorinda pushes that model toward its breaking point.[6] But doing so also may tempt us to downplay or ignore the ethical breaches that begin each of these three stories. Indeed, when we call the pain of those who suffer violence and the pain of those who inflict it by the same name, we risk neglecting the cries of victims, obscuring crucial questions of responsibility and blame, and forestalling efforts to heal and reconcile.

And yet we needn't do so. Avoiding these pitfalls begins by suggesting that while Pistorius, Kyle, and Tancred may suffer, some part of their pain is not "trauma." These three stories of men struggling in the wake of perpetration reveal not that the trauma model is broken—only that it has been stretched too thin. And this book is an effort to clarify the boundaries of trauma theory by introducing a new way to think about the pain that sometimes follows perpetration. Over the last decade or so, psychologists have proposed a new concept that helps us understand the unique ways an individual may suffer after breaching his or her own ethical code. That concept is called moral injury. (The term was coined by Jonathan Shay in the 1990s, but contemporary specialists have significantly expanded on his narrow definition of it.) Briefly, moral injury is the enduring psychic pain that may afflict someone who either commits or witnesses a significant moral transgression.

A majority of moral injury research comes out of the military setting, and much of it begins with two simple observations. The first of these is the basic fact that those who kill in war are more likely to suffer psychic pain than those who do not. As a case in point, David Wood cites the work of Shira Maguen, a VA psychologist who studies the effects of killing on combat veterans. According to Maguen, service members who kill in war are "twice as likely to develop frequent and severe psychological symptoms as those who had not" (*What* 14). Lieutenant Colonel Dave Grossman's *On Killing* advances a similar case. Grossman argues for the existence of a "powerful, innate human resistance toward killing one's own species" (xxxi), and he contends that breaking down that resistance takes a substantial psychological toll with long-lasting effects. Thus, he claims that the most prominent causes of lasting anguish for veterans include causing, witnessing, or commanding the death of others (86–89).

The second observation that leads to the concept of moral injury is the simple fact that service members who break their moral codes (or stand by as another does the same) exhibit symptoms that don't always fit existing psychological diagnoses. Both the service member who barely survives an IED blast and the one who accidentally shoots a child may be tormented by their experiences. Previously, we might have described both service members as "traumatized," but it turns out that they may exhibit different symptoms. As Wood writes, "We have come to group all these psychological injuries under the label 'PTSD.' That's wrong" (*What* 15).[7] The blast survivor may have nightmarish flashbacks of the explosion or a heightened startle reflex. The shooter, by contrast, may be irrationally angry, take unnecessary risks, or begin to question his or her own sense of goodness. This divergence exemplifies Edward Tick's claim that the pain of perpetration is a "characteristic wounding"; to elaborate, he cites a number of veterans who express their frustration at clinicians who fail to see this type of suffering as unique:

> "We were not innocent," Vietnam War Chaplain William Mahedy declared. "We were participants in evil" and "moral outrage." Tyler Boudreau complained that veterans are usually treated only like victims when they are simultaneously perpetrators and victims, each with its characteristic wounding. To express the depth and seriousness of this moral wound, Larry Dewey referred to "breaking the Geneva Convention of the soul." (151)

This last service member's striking phrase—"breaking the Geneva Convention of the soul"—is something close to what we now call moral injury.

Though I will go into greater depth explaining the clinical details of the concept in the following chapter, I offer what has become the standard definition of MI here. The language comes from a team of researchers led by Brett Litz, who has done pioneering work in this fledgling field; for Litz et al., moral injury is "the lasting psychological, biological, spiritual, behavioral, and social impact of perpetrating, failing to prevent, or bearing witness to acts that transgress deeply held moral beliefs and expectations" ("Moral" 697).[8] In brief, committing or witnessing a significant ethical breach may psychically wound. For the moment, it is worth noting the breadth of the definition. A moral injury might result from acts of commission or omission—and from wrongs perpetrated or merely observed. One should also realize that not all who do or experience wrong are morally injured. Like posttraumatic stress disorder, moral injury afflicts some and spares others. Clinicians have been able to identify some of the factors that will predispose an individual to such pain, and I outline some of these factors in the next chapter. But for now, suffice it to say that moral injury springs in part from an inability to contextualize a wrong.

To illustrate the point, we may return to the case of the service member who shoots a child. Most veterans would feel compunction in the wake of such an incident. But many would also be able to provide relevant background information that might help them move past the decision. For instance, they might say, "Yes, it is terrible that I killed a child. But the sun was at such an angle that my vision was fuzzy, the boy was roughly the same size as the men near him, and he was aiming an automatic weapon at my best friend." The morally injured individual has no such defenses, and the only explanation for the bad action is the rottenness of his or her soul. Wood explains the thought processes of the veteran Nik Rudolph to make the point: "Like all of us, Nik had always thought of himself as a good person. But does a good person kill a child? Follow that line of thinking, and it quickly becomes *No, a good person doesn't kill a child, therefore I must be a bad person. And think of all the other bad things I've done. . . . If I killed a child, could I ever be a trustworthy father*" (*What* 16). Note the slow slippage of evil in Rudolph's thinking: I did a bad thing; I am a bad person; I have always been a bad person; I could never be other than a bad person.

Morally injured individuals are unable to fence in the perceived ill effects of their actions, which take on the feel of a spreading soul infection. As we will see in the next chapter, some scholars call this sense that evil has slipped its bounds "demoralization"; others call it a "global negative evaluation of the self" (Katchadourian 16).[9]

I should make clear here that the moral injury construct does not foreclose on the possibility that those who unduly suffer in the aftermath of an ethical breach might not *also* suffer PTSD. As will become clear below and in chapters 1 and 5, moral injury's frequent coappearance with PTSD has made it difficult for specialists to isolate the effects of the former. I should also note that affirming such a coappearance significantly problematizes the hard distinction made frequently (if erroneously) in previous trauma-theoretical works between victims and perpetrators. Michael Rothberg traces the outlines of this problem in a previous discussion of Leys's critique of Caruth. In it, he argues, Leys

> elides the category of "victim" with that of the traumatized subject. . . . [W]hile one speaks conventionally, as Leys does, of a "victim of trauma," such a formulation of victimization has a different ontological status from the distinction between perpetrators and victims with which it is often confused. Thus, on the one hand, we can conceive of a victim who has not been traumatized—either because the victimization did not produce the kind of disruption that trauma ought to signify in order to have conceptual purchase, or because the victim has been murdered, as in the case of Clorinda. The dead are not traumatized, they are dead. (*Multidirectional* 90)

Such insights compel us to use these terms—victim and perpetrator—both carefully and sparingly, not only because a person is seldom just one or the other but also because we can imagine morally injured victims and traumatized perpetrators.[10] There are few better examples of such blurring than Primo Levi's discussion of the "gray zone" of the concentration camps in *The Drowned and the Saved*. In that volume, he speaks of the "moral collapse" that often breaks new arrivals as their hopes of allying themselves with other innocent "victims" are immediately dashed. Levi writes, "The network of human relationships inside the Lagers was not simple: it could not be reduced to the two blocs of victims and persecutors" (37).[11] That such a reduction never takes place is, for Levi, one of the most nefarious aspects of the camps, in which Nazis seek not merely to torture and kill inmates but also to "degrade" them by making them complicit in the camps' horrors: "It is naïve, absurd, and historically false to believe that an infernal system such as National Socialism sanctifies its victims: on the contrary, it degrades them, it makes them resemble itself, and this all the more when they are available, blank, and lacking a political or moral armature" (40). And as Levi is himself aware, the gray zone extends far beyond the bounds of Auschwitz, and it is often if not always impossible to divide the world into the "blocs" we expect to see there. In sum, in what follows, I seek wherever possible to heed Susannah Radstone's proviso that trauma specialists work past what she calls a "Manichean" distinction between "'victims' and 'perpetrators'" (19). I do, however, speak frequently of the pain of perpetration, which I take to be a rough synonym for moral injury.

It is also a worthwhile thing in these opening pages to begin situating moral injury with respect to longstanding discussions of moral emotions like shame and guilt. Scholars across the disciplines have long recognized such phenomena, and their writings can provide a helpful heuristic for understanding the unique ways that moral injury torments those it afflicts. In his book *Guilt: The Bite of Conscience*, Herant Katchadourian lays out a helpful taxonomy of moral emotions—for instance, embarrassment, guilt, shame, and regret. We find an analogue to MI in what Katchadourian calls "moral shame," one of whose defining characteristics is the global negative evaluation of the self. Katchadourian contrasts moral shame with plain old guilt—the normal, historically situated bad feeling that, for most, follows a bad act and then fades. For Katchadourian, the distinction between guilt and (moral) shame might come down to a simple shift in word emphasis: "guilt entails a specific act ('I *did* that horrible *thing*') whereas shame involves the whole self ('*I* did that horrible thing'). Hence, guilt has a more circumscribed effect on the person's sense of self while shame has a broader impact, engulfing the whole self ('I'm ashamed of who *I am*')" (24). Shame, it seems, will not be reined in.[12]

David Wood draws a similar distinction between guilt and shame—and sees the latter as a primary marker of moral injury. He writes that a guilty person might describe a moral error by saying, "I did a bad thing"; shame, however, might drive a person to draw a different conclusion from the same error: "I'm a bad person" (*What* 18). This sentence leads once again to what will become a familiar cul-de-sac, in which the morally injured individual cannot escape the sense of his or her own innate, enduring rottenness. The French writer Pascal Bruckner thinks of this state not in terms of shame but in terms of remorse, which he contrasts with repentance. For Bruckner, the latter indicates a healthy relationship with wrongdoing in which the sinner is able to both recognize and move past sin. On the other hand, remorse both gnaws and persists:

> Here we need to introduce a distinction, classic in philosophy, between repentance and remorse: the former recognizes the sin the better to separate itself from it and to enjoy the grace of convalescence, while the latter remains in sin out of a sick need to suffer its burning. Remorse does not repent of its sin; it feeds on it, wants to remain attached to it forever. (40)

When he engages the language of repentance, Bruckner adopts a religious vocabulary that may remind us of Christian discussions of sin. And at least one author—Brian S. Powers—has pointed out the family similarities between the Christian doctrine of original sin and moral injury. Accordingly, if moral injury is a new term, it touches upon or encompasses some very old ways of thinking about our emotional response to wrongdoing.

This insight forces us to grapple with the novelty of the term *moral injury*. If researchers claim that moral injury is a both a persistent aspect of the human condition and a natural (if lamentable) response to wrongdoing, why have we only begun discussing it since 2009? Or, in blunter terms, is moral injury a passing vogue—a psychological fad? Clinicians working on the concept propose a few reasons why we're just now acknowledging its effects. First, and as mentioned above, perhaps moral injury has not received much attention because it often coincides with PTSD.[13] Indeed, many veterans who serve long (or multiple) tours ultimately suffer from both, and clinicians have a hard time untwisting their individual coils.[14] Second, modern warfare (especially in the American setting) is much more likely to put the service member in a position where he or she will kill—a frequent trigger of MI. Brock and Lettini note that in World War II, nearly 75 percent of US service members did not fire directly at enemy troops (*Soul Repair* 17). Having learned this startling fact, US military leaders began putting service members through "reflexive fire training"—essentially a fire-first, think-second shooting technique. By the Vietnam era, 85 to 90 percent of US service members fired directly at the enemy (18). In citing these numbers, Brock and Lettini draw on the work of the army historian S. L. A. Marshall, whose pioneering work on US military fire rates changed the way we think about killing in war.

Grossman (who also draws on Marshall's research) devotes the first section of *On Killing* to demonstrating the increasing deadliness of war throughout history. He argues that the great battles of antiquity resulted in very few actual casualties; as an example, he suggests that Alexander the Great's confrontations with the enemy were likely little more than "bloodless pushing match[es]" (13). Indeed, it wasn't until the 1960s or so that a majority of US combat veterans would come home having killed another human. Additionally, contemporary guerrilla wars (like Vietnam) and counterinsurgency campaigns (like Iraq and Afghanistan) put reflexive-fire-trained service members in morally ambiguous situations more often (Litz et al., "Moral" 696). When fighters dress like civilians, when children wear suicide vests, and when enemy gunners hold infants, ethical action becomes even more difficult. Finally, as Wood points out, at least in the American context, we are sending younger and younger people to fight our wars for us.[15] This trend means that many teenagers are forced to navigate the "moral swamps" of our contemporary conflicts (*What* 83). In sum, modern wars are increasingly likely to put young, shoot-first-trained service members in morally untenable situations. The result is a spike in moral injury.

This spike has led not only to the acknowledgment of the concept but also to a blossoming of MI research in the fields of psychology and social work—much of which we will review in the subsequent chapter. But this jump in interest has also led to fledgling interdisciplinary efforts to bring the insights of moral injury to other fields of study. Brock and Lettini have turned a theological lens on moral injury (and moral recovery) in *Soul Repair* (2013), and offer a moral injury analysis of biblical narratives in *Exploring Moral Injury in Sacred Texts* (2017). Nancy Sherman subjects moral injury to philosophical analysis in her 2015 volume *Afterwar*. And in *Torture and Dignity* (2015), J. M. Bernstein looks at the effects of moral injury research on our understanding of political philosophy and gender violence. My book carries on in this tradition, and in it, we will look at ways in which insights borrowed from moral injury psychology might enhance our understanding of literary texts. Indeed, moral injury and its antecedents show up in a myriad of literary works, from the *Mahabharata* to Toni Morrison and from Shakespeare to Leslie Marmon Silko. This book is designed to supplement existing works of trauma theory by giving us a more precise set of tools for looking at literary depictions of psychic pain. As such, it is written under the banner of Geoffrey Hartman, a pioneering scholar in looking at trauma in literature. In an early essay in the field, Hartman argues that literature might prove invaluable in helping us "read the wound" of trauma—that novels, plays, poems, and stories might provide new insights into the nature and function of the psychic pains that hurt us most deeply (537). My hope is that this volume will serve a similar purpose with respect to moral injury. Existing trauma-theoretical works do an excellent job of helping us analyze depictions of PTSD. In these pages, I hope to provide a means of doing the same thing with the suffering of those who breach their own ethical codes.

Before we launch into specifics, I must elaborate on a few of this book's working assumptions: first, moral injury themes (if not moral injuries themselves) are present in a surprising array of world literary works; second, not every character who commits or witnesses an ethical breach suffers the pain that anticipates moral injury; third and finally, authors' insertion of such themes into creative literature often shapes (and misshapes) those texts' form and style. To the first of these, many narratives attest to the broad notion that ethical and criminal breaches may effect enduring anguish for perpetrators. (This assumption undergirds Jonathan

Shay's pathbreaking discussions of moral injury in Homer in *Achilles in Vietnam* and *Odysseus in America*.) As such, Cain, Judas, and Oedipus fit the bill; Lady Macbeth and Raskolnikov do too. And many other works imply or assert that sin can bring on conditions that we might now call mental illness. In *The Libation Bearers*, a play that addresses Clytemnestra's torment after the slaughter of her husband, the chorus warns of a "frenzy [that] goes through the guilty,/seething like infection, swarming through the brain" (Aeschylus 179). In Shakespeare's *King Lear*, the aging monarch worries that the wrongs he's done to his daughter Cordelia will eventually drive him out of his mind: "I did her wrong. . . . I will forget my nature. So kind a father. . . . O let me not be mad, not mad, sweet heaven" (14; I, v, 20, 27, 39). When Dinah first comes upon Hetty after the latter kills her child in *Adam Bede*, her first thought is that the crime has pushed Hetty past her wits' end; Dinah "thought suffering and fear might have driven the poor sinner out of her mind" (Eliot 589). And in Sartre's play *The Condemned of Altona*, Johanna claims that the war criminal Franz has been driven "raving mad" by his atrocities (56). And while I would not go so far as to confidently diagnose any one of these characters with moral injury, it is my belief and my hope that the vocabulary of MI yields a new set of tools for understanding and exploring their pain.

In trying these tools on a wide variety of poems, plays, epics, and novels, I follow the "genealogical" approach that Morris applies to trauma in his excellent "biography" of PTSD, *The Evil Hours*. In that book, Morris acknowledges that PTSD may be as much a "product of culture" as a "biological fact" (61). Thus, he is careful not to assert an unbroken, transcultural history for trauma, instead seeking its ancestors, its "historical antecedents" (61). Morris himself follows in the footsteps of Roger Luckhurst, who channels

Bruno Latour in treating trauma not as a transhistorical, transcultural scientific theory but as a "conceptual knot" that "succeeds through its heterogeneity rather than its purity" (*Trauma* 14). Luckhurst goes on to argue that trauma is an "exemplary conceptual knot whose successful permeation must be understood by the impressive range of the elements that it ties together and which allows it to travel to such diverse places in the network of knowledge" (14). To employ a genealogical approach is first to admit, for instance, that Freud's trauma and Richard McNally's trauma are not identical; yet it allows that their family similarity might permit us to put them in particularly productive conversation.

In the preface to a volume on the future of trauma studies, Rothberg endorses Luckhurst's approach, noting that "thinking genealogically about trauma is one essential means of opening it toward possible, alternative futures. Genealogical thinking loosens up the reified common sense that tends to cluster around concepts that achieve a rapid rise in popularity" ("Beyond" xi). And yet the genealogical approach entails an obvious challenge: if "heterogeneous" traumas are indeed unique, can we apply the same term to each? Is it indeed worthwhile to corral all of these family members in the same pen? Here again is Rothberg: "Trauma today is probably not the trauma of twenty years ago and certainly not the trauma of the early twentieth century. Yet the way we talk about trauma today and tomorrow will certainly bear the traces of those earlier layers of historical accretion" ("Beyond" xi). Simply put, family similarities between different iterations of trauma are not fortuitous but instead are indicative of a shared lineage whose continuity—even if it is not an identity—cannot be ignored.

All these things might be said of moral injury, so I contend that it is appropriate to pursue a similarly genealogical approach in studying its various incarnations. Hence, my efforts to engage its "antecedents" in early literature (especially in chapter 2) should not be understood as part of an effort to establish a continuous, global line of transmission for the concept. In other words, I do not claim that the moral sufferings of Cain, Hetty, and the Iraq War vet are identical. I do, however, see the pain of the biblical character and Eliot's heroine as tremors that anticipate the bursting forth of the moral injury concept in the last few decades. Yet if moral injury is, like trauma, best understood as a sort of conceptual knot, it is a tighter one. Trauma's modern history as a clinical term stretches back at least to Freud and Janet—and perhaps, Sütterlin argues, earlier—and encompasses a remarkable number of disparate voices; in sum, it is perhaps less a knot than a messy tangle. Moral injury is a younger, narrower term developed by a smaller number of researchers singing in tighter chorus. Accordingly, they have built a firmer foundation from which we might dive back into the literary past in search of depictions of MI and its antecedents.

Yet while moral injury themes manifest in a variety of literatures, not every character who commits a crime or crosses a moral line will suffer psychologically. As with trauma, moral injury afflicts some and spares others. (One passenger in a military transport hit by an IED may experience PTSD symptoms; another may not.) Or more to the point, for every Macbeth there is an Iago. But perhaps a less pat example is in order here. Rostam is the great warrior hero of Ferdowsi's Persian epic, *Shahnameh*. In perhaps the most wrenching episode of the sprawling work—one that closely resembles the encounter between Tancred and Clorinda in Tasso—Rostam faces the great champion Sohrab on the battlefield, not knowing the latter is his young son. After two rounds of fighting, Sohrab bests Rostam and readies his dagger for the killing blow. The wily Rostam, however, persuades the young man that tradition dictates that a fighter must fell his opponent twice before killing him. Sohrab relents before learning his error, and the text calls Rostam's act "unworthy" and a "trick" (208–9). When the two meet again, Rostam kills his child; he learns his rival's true identity only as the boy bleeds out. Few would seem more likely to suffer something like moral injury than Rostam, who uses guile and deception to slay his own son. Yet in the pages that follow, while Rostam grieves his offspring's death, his pain is temporary and appropriate; ultimately it brings closure and healing. A few books later, Rostam seems no longer to be weighed down by his error. He even goes so far as to cite the death of Sohrab as evidence of devotion to his ruler: "For that king's sake I killed my own son, and there never was such a strong, chivalrous, war-tried hero as Sohrab" (498). Though Rostam commits a moral breach nearly identical to (if not more distasteful than) Tancred's, his sin does not pursue him.

But for others, it does, and this book is on its first level an effort to identify salient literary examples of moral injury themes. Yet it is not only—and not even primarily—about diagnosis. Certainly, it is instructive to compare, for instance, troubled veterans of the Iraq War to the conflicted warriors of the Indian epic *Mahabharata*. But my broader claim involves structure and style, for moral injury shapes—or warps—literary form. In suggesting that depictions of moral injury are stylistically unique, I follow the lead of literary critics who argue that trauma inflects text in similarly identifiable ways. Often, trauma theorists are drawn to narrative because of a widely held assumption that trauma is— at least at the outset—unknowable or unspeakable. As Visser puts it, the "inaccessibility or 'unspeakability' of trauma" is "'received wisdom' in trauma studies" (274). In this characterization, trauma hits the psyche with such force that one is initially unable to communicate—or "claim," in Cathy Caruth's terminology—the experience. For Caruth and her many adherents, trauma forces itself on the mind "too soon, too unexpectedly, to be fully known and is therefore not [initially] available to consciousness" (*Unclaimed* 4). Often, the victim finds traumatic memory difficult to access and hard to describe. As Judith Herman writes in *Trauma and Recovery*, "As the [therapeutic] narrative closes in on the most unbearable moments, the patient finds it more and more difficult to use words" (177). Caruth echoes Herman in her interview with Geoffrey Hartman, noting that "normally one [thinks] of trauma as the absencing of the possibility of speech" ("Interview" 641).

Because trauma is so hard to know, remember, and speak about, critics who attend to it often emphasize textual lacunae. Thus, when Caruth engages Freud's writing about his escape from Vienna as the Nazis rose to power, she argues that his flight is evident only in what he does not say about it: "Freud's writing preserves history precisely within this gap in his text; and within the words of his leaving, words that do not simply refer, but . . . convey the impact of a history precisely as what *cannot be grasped* about leaving" (*Unclaimed* 21). The traumatic nature of Freud's departure is somehow beyond his grasp; thus, it is inscribed in the gaps in his prose. In similar fashion, Caruth's reading of trauma in Resnais's film *Hiroshima Mon Amour* circles around a similar narrative break, when the film's female lead experiences—or fails to fully experience—the death of her German lover: "Between the 'when' of seeing his dying and the 'when' of his actual death *there is an unbridgeable abyss, an inherent gap of knowing,* within the very immediacy of sight, the moment of the other's death" (*Unclaimed* 39; emphasis mine). Again, Caruth's reading of a trauma text focuses on an absence, a silence in the film that marks the inaccessibility of the woman's traumatic memory of her lover's passing.[16]

By contrast, moral injury at least sometimes manifests in literature in a quite different, even opposite fashion. If—as Caruth and others suggest—literary trauma is communicated via tropes such as lack, absence, and silence, moral injury is frequently excessive. This excess is directly related to the key symptom of MI explained above: demoralization, or the global negative evaluation of the self. For those who suffer moral injury, an evil that would otherwise be restricted to a particular moment in time and place in the universe breaks free of its boundaries and spreads, threatening to darken all aspects of the perpetrator's perspective. Georges Bataille's seminal insights on excess provide this book's theoretical foundation, and his writings—especially in *The Accursed Share* and *Literature and Evil*—help me describe the ways moral injury themes often inflect style in terms of excess. For Bataille, human energy on both the individual and communal levels is characterized in terms of excess. Moral injury taints this oversupply, rendering our abundant natural energies terrifying. I argue further that this excess manifests in what I see as three tropes of MI in literature: hyperbole, sublimity, and "signs of solitude."

I will fully explain all three in chapter 2, but I should note here that I do not see this list as comprehensive. Nor do I see all three of these tropes as necessarily appearing in all the literatures that address the persistent pain that sometimes follows the commission or witnessing of ethical breaches. In other words, this book does not aim to present any comprehensive theory of moral injury. Such a study is likely years off, because the clinical history of MI in its current incarnation is quite brief. With apologies to Jonathan Shay, whose excellent work is discussed at greater length below, that history begins with the 2009 publication of Brett Litz et al.'s recalibration of the term in an article entitled "Moral Injury and Moral Repair in War Veterans: A Preliminary Model and

Intervention Strategy." That article has inspired a flurry of interest in moral injury and its effects that continues to this day. And
while much valuable work has been done in more fully elaborating on the concept, much remains to be done, and many crucial
clinical questions have yet to be answered. This book, then, appears just roughly a decade into the clinical history of moral injury. (By contrast, Caruth's *Unclaimed Experience* [1996] appeared
over a century after Freud, Breuer, and Janet theorized a link between "hysteria" and trauma, nearly three decades after veterans
and women's rights activists resurrected the term in the late sixties
and early seventies, and sixteen years after PTSD was added to the
DSM.) Hence, my work here has modest aims, prime among them
the introduction of the term to literary scholars. It is my expecta-
tion and my hope that I and other scholars might further extend
the project as we continue to unravel the conceptual knot that is
moral injury in future years.

Yet before that unraveling can begin, we must delve deeper into
the recent wave of MI research. Thus, in the following chapter, I provide a review of recent clinical work on moral injury. This concept
has been developed and advanced by a small but productive group
of psychologists, most of whom work in the military setting. In that
chapter, I aim to explain what MI is, how it manifests, how it should
be categorized, and how we might treat it. Chapters 3, 4, and 5 apply
the model laid out in chapters 1 and 2 in extended readings of imag-
inative literature and start exploring some of the ethical questions
they raise. I understand each of these chapters as addressing a distinct type of what come to be known as PMIEs, or potentially morally injurious events: crimes of commission, crimes of omission, and
crimes that are witnessed (or, perhaps more specifically, ignored).

I begin in chapter 3 with an extended reading of Dostoevsky's
Crime and Punishment, which remains perhaps the most sustained,

focused meditation on the psychological aftereffects of a criminal act in all of world literature. This chapter both explores Raskolnikov's psychology through the moral injury lens and argues that in the figure of Sonya, Dostoevsky gives us a character who models some of the best practices contemporary researchers suggest for the treatment of MI. In the fourth chapter, I turn my attention to Albert Camus's *The Fall*, a novel that has already been claimed for trauma theory by Shoshana Felman. I argue, by contrast, that moral injury provides a more helpful paradigm for looking at Clamence's mental suffering; indeed, a discussion of the anguish that follows his failure to act (the crime of omission) allows us to begin thinking about the possibility of what we might call collective moral injury. The novel also raises the possibility that we are obligated to treat morally injured individuals who, because of their proximity to atrocity, could in recovery provide valuable testimony to mass trauma.

Chapter 5 looks at MI in the literatures of the recent US wars in Afghanistan and Iraq. I devote a chapter to these literatures in part because these wars have produced the bulk of recent MI research and in part because David Wood claims that moral injury is these conflicts' "signature wound." Accordingly, I argue that MI—and especially the pain associated with witnessing others' ethical breaches—is a pervasive presence in works by Brian Turner, Kevin Powers, Phil Klay, and Roy Scranton. I also argue in this chapter that stateside civilians' ignorance of (or failure to witness to) these conflicts is a contributing cause of service members' moral injury—and that these authors ask readers to ponder their own complicity in the wars fought in their name. In the coda, I turn to the question of ethics in wondering whether third parties have any formal responsibility to respond to the pain of the morally injured. In doing so, I propose a model for thinking about how we might witness to moral injury and how it might closely resemble trauma witness.

Notes

1. See especially Raya Morag's *Waltzing with Bashir: Perpetrator Trauma and Cinema*, which "seeks to theorize perpetrator trauma, a yet under-theorized field" (3). Less focused (but no less provocative) discussions of the theme from a variety of fields include Crisford et al., Papanastassiou et al., Rogers et al., Sindicich et al., and Taberner and Berger.

2. Alan Gibbs notes that trauma theorists have been "reluctant to acknowledge and therefore a little slow to examine" what he refers to as "perpetrator trauma" (166). Gibbs sees Dominick LaCapra as an exception to this trend but frets that LaCapra's discussions of it bely a "distaste for examining the phenomenon beyond a superficial level" (166). Though Gibbs himself writes a provocative chapter on perpetrator trauma in Gulf War memoirs, he admits that he uses the term "under erasure, for want of a better term" (200n.).

3. Giesen discusses the ways in which acknowledging citizens' (or citizen-soldiers') perpetration makes the process of communal identity formation difficult: "If a community has to recognize that its members, instead of being heroes, have been perpetrators who violated the cultural premises of their own identity, the reference to the past is indeed traumatic. The community can cope with the fundamental contradiction between identity claims and recognition only by a collective schizophrenia, by denial, by decoupling or withdrawal" (Alexander et al. 114). Seen in this light, *American Sniper* perfectly exemplifies such "denial."

4. In *History and Memory after Auschwitz*, Dominick LaCapra tells another story about "perpetrator trauma" and the ways the trauma model might obscure questions of collective moral responsibility. In March of 1985, Ronald Reagan was invited by Chancellor Helmut Kohl to a wreath-laying ceremony at Kolmeshohe Cemetery at Bitburg. It was quickly discovered that Kolmeshohe is home to the bodies of roughly four dozen SS members—along with approximately two thousand other German war dead (Weinraub, "Reagan"). That Reagan's team initially canceled a visit to a concentration camp on the same trip made for some ghastly optics: the US president appeared to be paying homage to Nazis while ignoring millions of their Jewish victims. A few weeks after announcing the trip, Reagan hosted the Holocaust survivor Elie Wiesel at the White House, where the latter was receiving the Congressional Gold Medal of Achievement. Wiesel used the opportunity to criticize the president's decision: "That place, Mr. President, is not your place. . . . Your place is with the victims of the SS" (Weinraub, "Wiesel"). Reagan did not take Wiesel's advice—though he did schedule a visit to Bergen-Belsen

on the same trip. Yet Reagan's decision to follow through with the visit to Kolme-shohe was somehow less disturbing than his rationale; defending his decision, he claimed that Nazism "victimized the whole world," adding, "I think that there is nothing wrong with visiting that cemetery where those young men are victims of Nazism also, even though they were fighting in German uniform, drafted into service to carry out the hateful wishes of the Nazis. They were victims, just as surely as the victims in the concentration camps" (quoted in LaCapra, *History* 60). Reagan's suggestion that the Nazis' suffering was somehow equivalent to that of Jews who died in the concentration camps is deeply troubling, and the clean confidence of Reagan's diction—"just as surely"—is even more problematic. Or, as LaCapra puts it, Reagan succumbed to a dangerously "indiscriminate gener-alization of victimhood, [a] homogenization of mourning" (*History* 60–61) that threatens to dilute or even dissolve the meaning of those words. The "danger" LaCapra isolates is the same one Mohamed sees in the Pistorius trial, just writ large: to speak of the victimization (or the traumatization) of Germans by the Führer is to sympathize with Nazis, to obscure their crimes, and to minimize the suffering of the Jews.

5. For more on Caruth's possible mischaracterization of Tancred as victim, see Di Prete, Hesford, Novak, Rothberg ("Beyond Tancred"), and Sicher. And for others who use the trauma model to treat perpetrator pain in literature, see Crownshaw, McGlothlin, Sanyal ("Torture"), Suleiman, Taberner, and Vice.

6. Writing of the so-called "Historians' Debate" in Germany, LaCapra identi-fies similar risks in what we might call trauma creep: "At times it indicates the problematic nature of the generalization of trauma and victimage to cover per-petrators in a manner that occludes the specificity of perpetrator trauma and even obfuscates the very existence or differential role of perpetrators who are transformed into victims" ("Revisiting" 84).

7. Drescher et al. elaborate on this claim. Many psychologists still believe that psychic suffering in the wake of war derives primarily from the stress of living for an extended period of time under the threat of harm or death; for Drescher et al., this consensus opinion is too simplistic (8).

8. In her book *Afterwar*, Nancy Sherman offers a parallel definition of moral injury that—while not so clinically grounded—is similarly evocative: "Roughly speaking, it refers to experiences of serious inner conflict arising from what one takes to be grievous moral transgressions that can overwhelm one's sense of goodness and humanity. The sense of transgression can arise from (real or appar-ent) transgressive commission and omissions perpetrated by oneself or others, or from bearing witness to intense human suffering and detritus that is part of the grotesquerie of war and its aftermath. In some cases, the moral injury has less to do with specific (real or apparent) transgressive acts than with a generalized sense of falling short of moral and normative standards befitting good persons and good soldiers" (8).

9. Katchadourian cites Helen Lynd to emphasize the tenacity with which this evaluation sticks to the self: "Shame is an experience that affects and is affected by the whole self. This whole-self involvement is one of its distinguishing characteristics. . . . One does not, as in guilt, choose to engage in a specific act. . . . Because of this over-all character, an experience of shame can be altered or transcended only in so far as there is some change in the whole self. . . . It is not an isolate act that can be detached from the self. . . . The thing that has been exposed is what I am" (quoted in Katchadourian 24–25). Because this revelation is so seminal and so wide reaching, June Price Tangney sees shame as a much more damaging emotion: "In shame, the focus of the negative evaluation is on the entire self. Following some transgression or failure, the entire self is painfully scrutinized and found lacking. . . . Guilt, in contrast, is a bad feeling, but it is a less global and devastating emotion than shame" (quoted in Katchadourian 25).

10. Rothberg continues elsewhere, "Trauma theory has helped us to think about the relation between perpetrators and victims. . . . But these categories alone are not sufficient to understand 'our' positioning in this globalized scenario of exploitation and trauma. Nor is the third term usually brought up at this point sufficient: the bystander. We are more than bystanders and something other than direct perpetrators in the violence of global capital. Rather, in he terms I have been developing in other contexts, we are *implicated subjects*, beneficiaries of a system that generates dispersed and uneven experiences of trauma and wellbeing simultaneously" ("Beyond" xv). Such reflections led him to publish a book-length study theorizing this new term: *The Implicated Subject: Beyond Victims and Perpetrators*. In it, he offers a more comprehensive definition: "Implicated subjects occupy positions aligned with power and privilege without being themselves direct agents of harm; they contribute to, inhabit, inherit, or benefit from regimes of domination but do not originate or control such regimes. An implicated subject is neither a victim nor a perpetrator, but rather a participant in histories and social formations that generate the positions of victim and perpetrator, and yet in which most people do not occupy such clear-cut roles. Less 'actively' involved than perpetrators, implicated subjects do not fit the mold of the 'passive' bystander, either" (*Implicated* 1).

11. To suggest that it is difficult simply to delineate the borders of these two "blocs" is not to suggest that there is a total breakdown of the distinction between victims and perpetrators in the camps. Accordingly, Leys takes issue with Agamben's argument that "in the gray zone *the positions of victim and oppressor are reversible or interchangeable*" (*Guilt* 158).

12. Se also Ruth Leys's provocative *From Guilt to Shame: Auschwitz and After*.

13. Litz et al. provide a helpful review of the ways our understanding of PTSD might cover some of the manifestations of MI ("Moral" 698).

14. Wood writes that moral injury "symptoms can be similar to those of PTSD: anxiety, depression, sleeplessness, anger" (*What* 17).

15. "In 2005, with American troops in desperate fights across Afghanistan and Iraq, 29 percent of enlisted marines on active duty hadn't yet celebrated their twenty-first birthdays. Include those who had just turned twenty-one, and the share of the young rises to 43 percent in the Marine Corps and 24 percent in the army. By 2007, with the wars demanding more manpower, the military services enlisted 7,558 seventeen-year-olds. . . . The Pentagon's total intake of seventeen-to twenty-year-olds that year was 86,072—more than half of all the men and women it recruited. And they finish at a young age: in 2010, for instance, half of marines and a quarter of army troops completed their enlistment term after serving four years. As under-twenty-five-year-olds with no experience as adult civilians, they returned to face daunting problems that would frustrate anyone with decades more wisdom and maturity" (Wood, *What* 28–29).

16. We see a similar trend developing in Caruth's interview with Geoffrey Hartman, which circles around an extended reading of the passage from Wordsworth's *Prelude* about the untimely death of the boy from Winander. In their interpretation of that poem, that which "cannot be grasped" about the child's passing falls into the space between two of the poem's stanzas ("Interview" 630 ff.).

1

Moral Injury

A CLINICAL PORTRAIT

In *Thank You for Your Service*, David Finkel traces the outlines of a full-blown mental health epidemic among military veterans returning from Afghanistan and Iraq. As of 2013, when his book was published, over two million men and women had been sent to one of those two wars—many repeatedly. (The Watson Institute at Brown University puts that number at 2.7 million as of early 2015.) And while many of these millions return to what look like normal lives, Finkel cites studies suggesting that between 20 and 30 percent suffer from either PTSD or traumatic brain injury (11). Simple math suggests, then, that upward of three-quarters of a million veterans of these two wars are currently living with the psychic pain of some sort of trauma. These numbers are staggering, but even more troubling is the fact that traditional treatment regimens seem to have little effect in helping these veterans cope with their pain. David Wood cites research by Brett Litz, Maria Steenkamp, and others suggesting that "the most widely used therapies for PTSD . . . [are] only marginally effective" (*What* 257). Indeed, some prominent treatment models—notably prolonged exposure (PE)—"did not lead to meaningful PTSD symptom reduction" at all (quoted in Wood, *What* 257). In sum, hundreds of thousands of veterans are plagued by mental illnesses, and we don't have good strategies to help them heal. This is the promise of the moral injury concept. Perhaps so many veterans continue to suffer because we haven't correctly identified the source of their pain, and perhaps MI is a significant contributing factor to it. Accordingly, researchers in the field believe that MI might be key to helping address a mental health crisis that continues to metastasize. In what follows, I review contemporary research on moral injury, outline working definitions of the term, identify common symptoms, and explain current possibilities for treatment.

The conflicts in Afghanistan and Iraq put moral injury on the map, but its history as a concept actually goes back to the decade before those wars began, to the work of Jonathan Shay. Shay's 1994 volume *Achilles in Vietnam* is a book-length effort to see what the *Iliad* can teach us about the psychology of the Vietnam veteran. Shay treats Homer's epic as a twenty-four-book exploration of the ancient military psyche and sees enlightening parallels between the ways twentieth-century Americans and eighth-century-BCE Greeks think about war and its effects. Crucial to this portrait is the service member's sense of betrayal—the lingering sense that his superiors have done grievous wrong, or done him wrong. One of the book's most evocative examples of such a betrayal is also one of its first; it comes from a Vietnam veteran:

> [W]ord came down [that] they were unloading weapons off them. Three boats. At that time we moved. It was about ten o'clock at night. We moved down, across Highway One along the beach line and took us [until] about three or four o'clock in the morning to get on line while these people are unloading their boats. And we opened up on them—aaah. And the fucking firepower was unreal, the firepower that we put into them boats. It was just a constant, constant firepower. It seemed like no one ever ran out of ammo. Daylight came [long pause], and we found out we killed a lot of fishermen

and kids. . . . The fucking colonel says, "Don't worry about it. We'll take care of it." Y'know, uh, "We got body count!" "We got body count!" So it starts working on your head. So you know in your heart it's wrong, but at the time, here's your superiors telling you that it was okay. So, I mean, that's *okay* then, right? (*Achilles* 4–5)

Yet even with the passage of time, the speaker—though he actually receives an award for participating in the "raid"—is haunted by his memory of it: "[H]e still feels deeply dishonored by the circumstances of its official award for killing unarmed civilians on an intelligence error. He declares that the day it happened, Christmas Eve, should be stricken from the calendar" (4).

In the years following that Christmas Eve, this veteran (and others put in similar situations) suffers a variety of ill effects: rage, withdrawal, distrust, despair, and the creeping suspicion that neither he nor the world in which he lives is good. It is stories like these that compel Shay to develop an initial definition of moral injury. For Shay, moral injury occurs when one witnesses an authority figure breaching what the Greeks called *thémis*, which Shay translates loosely as "what's right": "When a leader destroys the legitimacy of the army's moral order by betraying 'what's right,' he inflicts manifold injuries on his men" (*Achilles* 6). Shay adopts the Greek term because he draws examples of moral injury both from the accounts of Vietnam veterans and from Homer's *Iliad*. Vietnam veterans might suffer from moral injury when a commanding officer repeatedly sends a grunt he doesn't like out on the most dangerous patrols. And Achilles is morally injured when Agamemnon steals the war spoils Achilles rightfully earns (13). In Shay's characterization, moral injury most frequently results in isolation and violent rage.

However, his definition of moral injury, situated as it is in the space between military superior and soldier, is relatively narrow.

Thus, in 2009, Litz et al. began testing the broader, more clinically grounded version of the term mentioned in the introduction. To review, for Litz et al., moral injury is "the lasting psychological, biological, spiritual, behavioral, and social impact of perpetrating, failing to prevent, or bearing witness to acts that transgress deeply held moral beliefs and expectations" ("Moral" 697). They argue that moral injury may result from a variety of different types of experiences, among them

> participating in or witnessing inhumane or cruel actions, failing to prevent the immoral acts of others, as well as engaging in subtle acts or experiencing reactions that, upon reflection, transgress a moral code. We also consider bearing witness to the aftermath of violence and human carnage to be potentially morally injurious. (700)

Litz et al.'s definition of MI expands on Shay's in a variety of ways.[1] First and most importantly, they characterize moral injury as occurring not only when one witnesses an ethical breach, but also when one commits or fails to stop one.[2] In the intervening years, researchers have pointed out that early discussions of moral injury often featured a conflation of event and aftereffect—a confusion as to whether "moral injury" refers to a discrete incident or the psychic pain that lingers in its wake. To sort out this confusion, a number of scholars have introduced terminology to make the distinction clearer. Accordingly, Farnsworth et al. distinguish between moral injury and "morally injurious events," or MIEs ("Functional" 392). Litz and others prefer PMIEs, or "potentially morally injurious events."[3] Both of these, however, are distinct from moral injury, which describes the deleterious aftereffects of MIEs or PMIEs.

Of course, Litz et al.'s expanded definition might lead us to a crucial secondary question: what exactly are morals? Both Shay and

Litz et al. offer helpful descriptions. Shay's definition—roughly, "what's right"—is attractive in its brevity and its flexibility. Litz et al. offer a lengthier, more nuanced definition of the term:

> Morals are defined as the personal and shared familiar, cultural, societal, and legal rules for social behavior, either tacit or explicit. Morals are fundamental assumptions about how things should work and how one should behave in the world. For example, the implicit belief that "the world is benevolent" stems from the expectation that others will behave in a moral and just matter. Another tacit assumption is that "people get what they deserve"; thus, if someone does not act within the accepted moral code, a punishment should ensue. ("Moral" 699)

A few aspects of this longer description deserve attention. First, Litz et al. point out that moral codes can be either "shared" or "personal"; they can be widely held social norms or more specific individual creeds. Thus, moral injury might result from the killing of a child—an act all but universally considered unethical. Or it might follow the breach of a much more idiosyncratic individual ethic. Second, one should note that the second component of Litz et al.'s definition—regarding "fundamental assumptions about how things should work"—is essentially metaethical. In other words, though moral injury might occur when one breaks a rule, it might also occur when the very structure of morality seems to be under assault. As an example, we return for a moment to the story of the Vietnam veteran with which this chapter opens. Part of that service member's discomfort springs from the fact that those involved in the massacre are given medals for their involvement. An act that should result in severe punishment instead entails acclaim and honor. Here, it appears to the speaker as if the very fabric of morality is in danger.

That being said, there is a sense in which finding a discrete definition of morality in this context is beside the point because what is most crucial in moral injury research is the individual's perception of a moral breach. Briefly, moral injury can occur only if a person *believes* he or she has broken some deeply held moral code. As Litz et al. write, "The individual also must be (or become) aware of the discrepancy between his or her morals and the experience (i.e., moral violation), causing dissonance and inner conflict" ("Moral" 700). Thus, in the first widely used survey for measuring the phenomenon—the Moral Injury Events Scale—Nash et al. don't ask respondents about specific transgressions; they write, "The MIES indexes only *perceived* contradictions between remembered behaviors and post hoc moral expectations in the necessarily complex moral context of modern warfare; it does not index wrongdoing in any form" (650). Accordingly, the researchers ask respondents only to agree or disagree with relatively general statements, such as "I saw things that were morally wrong," "I violated my own morals by failing to do something that I felt I should have done," or "I feel betrayed by leaders who I once trusted" (651).

Yet to make these observations is not to claim that moral injury is a totally subjective category. Indeed, existing research notes a number of experiences that are more likely to morally injure. In a series of studies, research teams led by Shira Maguen have found a strong correlation between the act of killing in war and trauma symptoms—among them symptoms associated with moral injury. Other groups have been more specific. Litz et al. identify a number of other wartime experiences that often seem to be morally injurious—some of which occur with higher frequency in urban and guerrilla conflicts like the US wars in Iraq and Afghanistan. Among them are killing a civilian who is mistaken for an insurgent, seeing or handling human remains, being unable to help sick or wounded women and children, or being directly responsible for the death of an enemy combatant ("Moral" 697). Drescher et al. add to this list leadership failures and within-rank violence (including sexual assault). (Flipse Vargas et al. largely agree.) Currier et al. argue that while "killing and atrocities are certainly stressors that can warrant careful clinical attention," other events "could have significant mental health consequences" ("Initial" 55). Thus, they develop an updated moral injury survey that includes things like survivor guilt, friendly-fire accidents, acting out of vengeance or the enjoyment of violence, or perceiving the humanity of an enemy.

To suggest that there are a number of events that often morally injure, however, is not to suggest that all are equally likely to do so. Clinicians argue that there is a "dose-response" relationship between the intensity of the experience (in terms of either severity or duration) and the likelihood of moral injury (Murray et al.). For example, a service member who accidentally fires a rocket-propelled grenade into an orphanage is at greater risk of moral injury than one who accidentally injures a noncombatant. And a veteran who serves four tours in Iraq is at greater risk than one who serves just one.

Of course, all of these studies are based on work with veterans; unsurprisingly, then, our understanding of moral injury is shaped by the experience of service members in wartime. However, other recent work has sought to apply the paradigm outside the military setting. For instance, Nash and Litz argue that the moral injury model might be helpful for understanding the psychic suffering of not only veterans but also the families of returning service members; they articulate a "potential adaptation of that model to military spouses and children, taking family systems and developmental stages into account" (366). Moving farther afield,

McCormack and Riley see moral injury in police officers medically discharged because of traumas they suffered on the job. The injury here occurs when officers come to recognize that "they had believed and enthusiastically committed to an organization . . . which now rejected them. They felt betrayed" (24). In another vein, Haight et al. look at the prevalence of moral injury among those working in child protection services. Their work suggests that workers in this field both see and suffer moral injury with some regularity. For example, both parents and clinicians may be morally injured by a parent's abuse or negligence. And case workers may also suffer moral injury "as a result of under-resourced systems. They described challenges related to high caseloads and lack of resources, unfair laws and policies, . . . systemic biases, harm to children by an inadequate foster care system and poor quality social services" (109). In sum, while the lion's share of MI research has taken place in the military setting, scholars are confident that the paradigm has use value in civilian psychology as well.

Since the publication of Litz et al.'s study, a number of other teams have published work both corroborating and elaborating on it. Three pieces in particular—published by teams led by Drescher, Flipse Vargas, and Farnsworth, respectively—help us better understand the symptoms of moral injury. I have divided these symptoms into four clusters for the purposes of simplicity and clarification.[4] However, it is important to acknowledge that moral injury—like trauma—is not a monolith. MI manifests in a multitude of ways, and those who suffer it exhibit different arrays of symptoms appearing in varying intensities. That being said, its manifestations do follow a number of regular patterns. First, research backs up Shay's suggestion that moral injury may lead to both anger and social isolation. Litz et al., Flipse Vargas et al., and Farnsworth et al. see anger and aggression as linked to the feelings of shame resulting from the moral breach. As an example, we might turn to a story Nancy Sherman tells about a psychiatrist named Sam. In the years following the Vietnam War, Sam works with a veteran, "Bill," who feels ashamed of his service: "[I]n Bill's own eyes, 'he was a murderer,' whose deeds in war were ultimately unjustified" (48). This lingering feeling often threatens to manifest itself as "raging resentment," and Sam occasionally fears for his life: "I was always very cautious about making him too angry, and at times my blood ran cold when I realized that he could kill me without a weapon at any time. . . . The work involved this fear that he had at all times that he could, if made angry, kill again or he could kill those responsible for being in the war" (48). Such rage is not only dangerous; it is maladaptive, as it drives away family, friends, and others who might provide help.

Litz et al. argue that such aggression often coincides with other relational problems, including "toxic interpersonal difficulties" and "decreased empathy for others" ("Moral" 699). These may drive the morally injured individuals to isolate themselves. Drescher et al. assert that such habits may be exacerbated by morally injured individuals' "reduced trust in others and in social/cultural contracts" (9). This diminished trust often accompanies shame, which Farnsworth et al. note often activates "social hiding behaviors" ("Role" 251). And Litz et al. posit that social isolation may also result from the community's tendency to distance itself from perceived criminals: "[T]hose who suffer from moral injury may be more reluctant to utilize social supports, and it is possible that they may be actually shunned in light of the moral violation" ("Moral" 699). For example, Jeffrey Lucey, an Iraq veteran, writes to his girlfriend of his experience, "I've seen and done enough horrible things to last me a lifetime" (Iraq Veterans 158). His parents report that, on returning from the Middle East, Jeffrey is uncharacteristically reserved: "Our marine physically returned to us, but his spirit died somewhere in Iraq." When he tries to tell stories of his time in country, they all end with a similar refrain: "You could never understand" (160). And when he spends time with his girlfriend, she finds him "distant"; on a getaway to Cape Cod, "he didn't want to walk on the beach. He later told a friend at college that he'd seen enough sand to last a lifetime" (158). He is eventually able to confide in his grandmother, but he can only explain to her a ubiquitous sense of isolation; he confesses, "You could be in a room full of people, but still feel so alone" (158).

Nancy Sherman notes the ways that social isolation might be linked with a certain carelessness with one's own life; she explains that MI can lead to "indifference to life and death [which] is also indifference to social connection" (11). It is unsurprising, then, that a third cluster of MI symptoms groups around poor treatment of the self, including lacking self-care, self-handicapping, self-harm, and even suicide (Drescher et al. 9). In their milder incarnations, such phenomena may manifest in behaviors such as "retreating in the face of success or good feelings"; more troubling versions include drug and alcohol abuse (Litz et al., "Moral" 701). Tick is one of many who writes about how morally injured people self-medicate with drugs and alcohol. As an example, he tells the story of Vince, a combat infantryman who binge drinks to control the pain from his memories of war. Often fine for weeks at a time, Vince occasionally holes up in a motel room with bottles of brown liquor: "They only want me to control my drinking," he explains. "Don't they understand that I can't stop drinking as long as the war is locked up inside me?" (110). Of course, such behavior can be dangerous for both the drinker and others. Vince eventually has his license taken away after three DUI convictions. Jeffrey Lucey, mentioned above, also develops a severe drinking problem after his return. The first day he seeks help from local VA administrators, he blows a 0.328 blood alcohol content at the office and is involuntarily committed for four days. Around the same time, he additionally starts abusing Klonopin and Prozac (Iraq Veterans 157).

Sometimes morally injured individuals are reckless with their lives and health in other ways. In *Afterwar*, Sherman mentions the death of Matt Tooker, who witnesses the killing of at least two fellow service members on a roof in Afghanistan. Tooker himself makes it home alive but dies later in a motorcycle accident that his friend TM is "pretty sure . . . was the culmination of risky, suicidal behavior" (24). To wit, "risky" acts are often indistinguishable from parasuicidal or suicidal behaviors. For Brock and Lettini, these are the moral injury's scariest incarnations: "One of the most dangerous aspects of moral injury is the collapse of meaning and the loss of a will to live" (80). In the weeks and months following his return, Jeffrey Lucey's friends and family slowly come to learn that he has lost that will. One day, he shows his sister a rope and a tree he fantasizes about using to kill himself. Later on, he goes out for doughnuts and totals the car under suspicious circumstances. His parents write, "Was it a suicide attempt? We're never going to know" (Iraq Veterans 159). Shortly thereafter, Jeffrey hangs himself in his parents' basement. Marine rifleman Sergio Kochergin tells a similar story about one of his fellow service members. Sergio's company is stationed near the Syrian border and gets in the habit of using "drop weapons," seized guns that allow his company to skirt the rules of engagement in hostile territory; the guns, Sergio says, "were given to us by our chain of command in case we killed somebody without weapons so that we would not get into trouble" (Iraq Veterans 50). This process allows his company to cover up the murder of many innocent civilians, and memories of it haunt them. Later on, back in the United States, one of his roommates is put on suicide watch on and off for a few months. But according to Sergio, "A week before a family day he was released from the watch so that he would not say anything to his parents and he did not say anything to them. About a month into the deployment he blew his brains out in one of the shower stalls" (51).

Poor self-care in both its milder and more fatal incarnations is often driven by a fourth cluster of MI markers: increasingly negative feelings about the moral value of self and world—an attitude some clinicians call "demoralization." (As previously mentioned, Katchadourian calls it "global negative evaluation" of the self.) First, the morally injured often come to see *themselves*—rather than the acts they commit—as bad, evil, or morally degraded. They are less likely to think they have done bad things and more likely to believe they are bad people. As Litz et al. put it, "[T]he more time passes, the more service members will be convinced and confident that not only their actions, but *they* are unforgiveable" ("Moral" 700). Accordingly, David Wood tells the story of Civil War–era doctors who are befuddled by the case of a Union infantryman named Peter Reed, who believes "he was guilty of great crimes. . . . [H]e thinks he is lost for all eternity" (*What* 121).

More troubling, perhaps, is the tendency of the morally injured to begin to see not only themselves but also the world as irretrievably unethical. As an example, Brock and Lettini cite the eulogy delivered at the funeral of a military suicide: "He thought the world was supposed to be a better place than it is" (48). Litz et al. attest to the ways a bad feeling about the self might morph into bad feelings about the world in general: "An individual with moral injury may begin to view him or herself as immoral, irredeemable, and un-reparable *or believe that he or she lives in an immoral world*" ("Moral" 698; emphasis mine). The sense that the world itself is immoral may then lead to increasing skepticism about spirituality or the promises of religion. Brock and Lettini note that the morally injured often feel as if a "profound spiritual crisis . . . has changed them, perhaps beyond repair" (51). This sense of spiritual crisis may affect either the believer or the God in whom he or she believes. Brock and Lettini quote a military chaplain, many of whose clients "felt that they had committed a personal affront against God" (26). By contrast, Drescher et al. see "negative attributions about God" in their work with the morally injured (9). In sum, those suffering moral injury sometimes feel that they have let God down; others believe God has let them down.

In *Soul Repair*, Brock and Lettini tell the story of Camilo, who suffers some of these symptoms after his return from Iraq. Camilo arrives in country shortly before the "shock and awe" campaign of 2003 and is quickly overtaken by new beliefs about the immorality of the overall war effort. He characterizes the Americans' heavy, indiscriminate bombings of the country as a violation of international law and suggests that no one could appropriately process the death of innocents on such a scale: "Nothing ever prepares you for going to Iraq and seeing the destruction of an entire nation. Nothing ever prepares you for . . . the unmeasured killing of civilians, nothing ever prepares you for what that does to you as a human being . . . to kill an innocent person" (33). Unfortunately, Camilo eventually has a more personal experience with the killing of a civilian. When his unit is pressured by a group of protesters to take shelter in a vacant building, Camilo catches sight of an adolescent on the edges of the crowd holding what looks like a grenade. Ordered to fire, he squeezes off eleven rounds, dropping the boy cold. Later on, he observes prisoners of war degraded and abused. These and other experiences lead him to an acute sense of demoralization. He traces the change back to the day he shot the boy: "That day I knew something had forever changed inside me. I felt a hole within me that had no bottom, an infinite void that could never be replenished" (88). This "change" is the subtle creep of demoralization: Camilo doesn't *do* something evil on that day; he *becomes* something evil. This change has both philosophical and practical effects. At one level, Camilo comes to question his humanity and worries that a longer stay in the war zone will hollow him out entirely: according to Brock and Lettini, "He was afraid that if he [stayed], he would lose his soul and never be human again" (62). He also begins to doubt his ability to raise and support his daughter: "[H]e started questioning his ability to be a good father after what he had done in war. . . . 'How could I ever teach my daughter right from wrong when I had done so wrong myself? What moral authority did I have left to be a good father?'" (61). Moral injury threatens the integrity of the self and may send one spiraling into despair and self-accusation.

Of course, not everyone who commits, witnesses, or learns of an immoral act will exhibit all—or any—of these four clusters of symptoms. Thus, Litz et al. also identify two "cognitive vulnerabilities" that may make an individual more likely to exhibit symptoms of moral injury. One is "rumination": passively, repeatedly thinking about negative events and emotions ("Moral" 699). A second is "negative attributional style," which the researchers describe as "consistently attributing negative events to internal, stable, and global causes" (699). They go on to define these three terms as follows: "*global* (i.e., not context dependent), *internal* (i.e., seen as a disposition or character flaw), and *stable* (i.e., enduring; the experience of being tainted)" (700). In somewhat more straightforward terms, a person with a negative attributional style might see a moral breach not as connected to a particular time and place but instead as possible no matter the context (global); he or she might see that moral breach as resulting not from a momentary decision but from an enduring problem with his or her own character (internal); and he or she might see the moral breach not as fleeting but as having lasting—perhaps eternal—effects (stable).

Though much promising research has been done on moral injury—on its shape and symptoms, its dangers and its therapeutic promise—it is still a relatively new concept, and even though Litz and Kerig note that MI has garnered "international recognition" (341) in the 2010s, those who champion its usefulness are still pushing for wide acceptance in the broader psychological community. Accordingly, Drescher et al. conducted a moral injury survey with the participation of roughly two dozen religious leaders, academic researchers, clinicians, and policymakers with specialties in trauma. Summing up their results, they write, "There was unanimous agreement that the concept of 'moral injury' is useful and needed. . . . There was also universal agreement that the construct of moral injury was not fully encompassed by the PTSD diagnosis criteria and its related features" (11). Such unanimity suggests that mental health specialists would be well served to begin treating moral injury as a unique experience.

But what type of experience? While there is a growing consensus that moral injury is a useful term, specialists disagree about the best way to categorize the experience. Litz et al., for example, do not argue for a new diagnostic category ("Moral" 696), and few are willing to call moral injury a novel *diagnosis*. Drescher et al. call it a "construct" (8). Wisco et al. identify it as a "unifying construct" (341) and a "modifiable risk factor for mental disorder" (346) but argue that more work is necessary before we can "establish diagnostic criteria" (346). Many (including Litz et al. ["Moral"] and Nash et al.) simply call moral injury a "concept" (as I usually do here) and attempt to situate it within the constellation of traumatic or paratraumatic experiences. Flipse Vargas et al. argue that many moral injury themes "fall outside the purview of the diagnostic criteria for PTSD"; nonetheless, they retain the language of trauma in characterizing such themes as "unique sets of reactions to traumatic experiences" (248). And by the time Litz comes back around to write *Adaptive Disclosure* in 2016, he and his research team essentially describe moral injury as a unique flavor of trauma. I am not qualified to weigh in on such debates. But suffice it to say that I follow Drescher et al. in affirming that "there are uniquely morally injurious experiences in war and that these experiences create an array of psychological, spiritual, social and behavioral problems" (11).

Yet to situate moral injury within the orbit of trauma may again cause some to question its uniqueness. Nonetheless, researchers have come up with a variety of compelling reasons to see MI as a distinct concept despite its family relationship with PTSD. First, many identify PTSD symptoms that do not show up in the MI profile. Farnsworth et al. note that some "classic symptoms of PTSD have not yet demonstrated strong connections to moral injury," and draw specific attention to hyperarousal and hypervigilance—which have "been more tightly connected to fear" ("Functional" 393). Wood adds to this list flashbacks and memory loss (*What* 16). Approaching the problem from the other direction, Bryan et al. draw up a list of MI outcomes that don't correlate with a PTSD diagnosis: "[S]ocial problems, spiritual and/or existential issues, self-deprecation, problems with forgiveness, inability to trust others, anhedonia, anger/aggression, and embitterment have all been described and empirically examined, but are not considered central features of PTSD" (37).[5] As such, they propose the following diagram to help distinguish between the outcomes of PTSD and MI (figure 1).

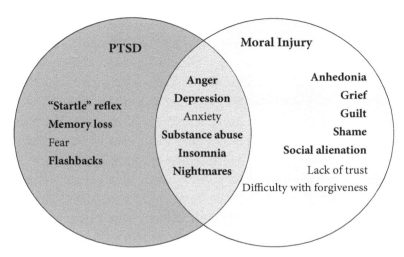

FIGURE 1
Diagram reproduced from Craig J. Bryan et al., "Moral Injury, Posttraumatic Stress Disorder, and Suicidal Behavior among National Guard Personnel," *Psychological Trauma: Theory, Research, Practice, and Policy* 10.1 (2018): 37. © 2017 American Psychological Association.

Further, Farnsworth et al. contend that even when PTSD and MI symptoms coincide (as they do in the middle part of figure 1 above), they serve different purposes in different populations; more simply, they have unique functions. As an example, they point to the fact that both traumatized individuals and morally injured individuals might isolate themselves; they write, "[B]oth moral injury and PTSD may elicit avoidance of public spaces, however the symptom function differs. PTSD avoidance serves to assuage safety concerns while avoidance in moral injury may be related to avoiding shame or 'exposing others to evil'" ("Functional" 393).

If it is necessary to discuss the often subtle distinctions between moral injury and trauma, it is equally important to distinguish the concept from widely discussed moral emotions such as shame and guilt—especially given the fact that early efforts to describe moral injury list feelings like these as symptoms. Farnsworth et al. are especially helpful in this respect, as they develop a clear distinction between what they call moral pain (e.g., shame, guilt, and anger) and moral injury. The feelings associated with moral pain, they argue, are both healthy and adaptive responses to either the commission or the witnessing of a transgressive act. In their words, moral pain "is to be understood as an expected, natural, and non-pathological consequence of exposure to MIEs" ("Functional" 392). Moral injury, by contrast, is an inability to cope with feelings like shame and guilt; it is, in their reworked definition, "expanded social, psychological, and spiritual suffering stemming from costly or unworkable attempts to manage, control, or cope with the experience of moral pain" (392). This definition recalls earlier efforts to distinguish PTSD from fear: if trauma is a healthy fear response stuck in overdrive, moral injury is shame or guilt stuck in overdrive.

If one accepts the existence of moral injury as a concept that is distinct from both trauma and moral pain—as an increasing number of specialists both in and outside the military community do—one must then wrestle with another crucial question: how do we treat it? Will morally injured individuals respond to routine treatments for other psychic maladies, like PTSD? Or do we need a unique treatment model? These debates are far from settled, but two sides are coalescing: those who believe that existing treatment regimes suffice and those who argue that this new concept demands a unique approach.

In a 2018 article, Held et al. argue that moral injury responds to two well-worn PTSD treatments: prolonged exposure (PE) and cognitive processing therapy (CPT). Prolonged exposure essentially asks clients to return repeatedly to the traumatizing (or morally injurious) moment in an effort to habituate themselves to the various discomforts it may inspire. David Finkel describes habituation with the help of one veterans' group session leader:

> The first time you see a scary movie, at least for me, it sucks. I get home, and I have nightmares, and I'm frustrated, and I don't sleep well. . . . The tenth time I see that scary movie, I'm, like, O.K., cue Freddy Krueger, here's the cheerleader who gets her neck cut off, here's the blood, and now the chainsaw, and I'm getting bored. It's the same principle with explosions for you guys. If you guys can go to a place and have the experience repeatedly, and stay with it until it starts to dissipate, that's when the explosion starts to be less and less impactful. It's called habituation. (59)

In the simplest terms, the more one is exposed either to memories of discrete horrors or to situations that recall them, the less potent—and disruptive—they ultimately are. Held et al. explain that prolonged exposure aims to reduce two of the most deleterious effects of PTSD: "avoidance and erroneous beliefs about oneself, others, and the world" (378). However, they argue that morally injured individuals exhibit essentially the same behaviors; therefore, PE is a valid and helpful treatment strategy for both conditions. Accordingly, they tell the story of "Carlos," a veteran who was compelled to shoot and kill a civilian girl he had previously befriended. (Insurgents wired her with a bomb and sent her in the direction of Carlos's company.) His therapy includes two types of exposure: imaginal, in-therapy exposure to memories of the event itself, and in vivo, "real-life" exposure to activities that recall the event (e.g., going to the park with his nieces). Held et al. argue that the first of these helps Carlos reduce "painful emotions associated with the memory and [helps] integrate more contextual detail in his memory, perhaps making it possible to reappraise his role" (383). Further, the in vivo exposure targets his "isolation and self-hatred by collaborating with the veteran to engineer experiences that may have provided corrective emotional experiences" (383).

Cognitive processing therapy offers a different approach. CPT takes as one of its starting points the notion that traumatized individuals have erroneous beliefs about the trauma itself; in the treatment's parlance, these beliefs are called "stuck points" (Held et al. 384). Held et al. give as an example a veteran who—experiencing violent combat—comes to believe (falsely) that "[t]he whole world is not safe at all" (380). They explain, "CPT uses cognitive restructuring techniques to promote the examination of these beliefs and the discovery of evidence that disproves stuck points. By doing so, individuals are able to more accurately evaluate the traumatic event and appropriately assign responsibility and blame" (380). Some morally injured individuals, they argue, are similarly "stuck"—and thus respond similarly to cognitive processing therapy. One service member who benefits significantly from CPT is "David," a veteran who shot and killed distant children suspected of digging holes for improvised explosive devices. (David acted under orders and within the rules of engagement.) David is caught up on a number of stuck points, one of which is particularly relevant to our articulation of the moral injury concept: "I am a monster" (386). Through the use of cognitive processing techniques and with the help of his therapist, David is able to realize that his behavior in the moment was not "monstrous": he didn't want to shoot the children, he tried to come up with ways to avoid the order, he tried to aim wide, and he felt great remorse after the shooting. Such realizations help David move past his maladaptive and ultimately false sense of his own "monstrosity."

But what if one's acts truly are monstrous? One can argue that in high-stress moments, Carlos and David were presented with a variety of untenable options; each selected the least bad path. What if David had gone hunting Iraqi civilians the night after a particularly bloody firefight? What if Carlos had raped a fellow service member? Would PE and CPT be similarly effective in helping them cope? Some scholars say no. The argument goes something like this: prolonged exposure and cognitive processing therapy help restore order in a life where only the illusion of disorder persists. Carlos and David suffer from false or exaggerated feelings of shame or guilt, and traditional therapies help either correct or contextualize these feelings. Yet some transgressive acts are more pointedly transgressive, and deep feelings of guilt and shame might be quite appropriate in their aftermath; contextualizing or correcting these feelings might therefore be *inappropriate*. Gray et al. think that this may be especially true of CPT. They write, "There are instances in which inordinately distressing cognitions are not errant, but rather, may well be reasonable and appropriate" (383). They go on to contend that "challenging the accuracy of self-blame in such cases is conceptually problematic and potentially harmful. Such an approach is based on a questionable premise—i.e., that self-blame and resulting guilt are inherently illogical or inaccurate. Though this is often the case, it is not invariably so" (383). The worry in such cases is that any relief that CPT brings may be either short lived or a sham.

Elsewhere, Litz et al. call efforts to contextualize (and hence acclimate oneself to) the memory of transgressive acts "moral reassurance" (*Adaptive* 16). (They also claim that both CPT and PE have contextualization as one of their most prominent aims.) In cases like David's and Carlos's, prolonged exposure and cognitive processing therapy help produce moral reassurance by providing

convincing—and healing—rationalizations for seemingly unethical actions. For Litz et al., classic examples include lines like
"'I did the best I could,' 'They didn't mean to hurt me,' or 'Look
at all the things I do right'" (16). But like Gray et al., Litz et al.
believe that moral reassurance isn't always an acceptable path in
the wake of moral injury: "We suggest that for some war zone
transgressions, moral reassurance might provide only short-lived
relief or at worst feel disingenuous to service members. This is
because moral reassurance cannot negate or invalidate troubling
and painful moral truths, though it can serve as a distraction"
(16–17). In such cases, they prefer creating the conditions for
an alternate process they refer to as "moral repair." Unlike moral
reassurance, moral repair does not seek to reintegrate the transgressive act into some "normal" system of understanding or perception; rather, it admits the deeply disruptive quality of some
transgressions and seeks something closer to forgiveness—or
self-forgiveness. Moral repair, they suggest, "must involve acceptance of inconvenient truths, after drawing them into as objective a focus as possible" (17). They call their preferred vehicle
for moral repair "adaptive disclosure" and argue that it "attempts
to help the patient integrate the discomfort of the moral injury
through experiencing forgiveness, self-compassion, and engaging in reparative behaviors" (17).

Litz et al. believe that adaptive disclosure is a promising treatment regimen for a variety of traumas but argue that it is uniquely
helpful for moral injury. It does feature an exposure piece that
readies the client to speak openly about the morally injurious
event. However, treatment does not end with exposure. Rather,
exposure prepares the client for a set of exercises intended to enable moral repair. The most crucial of these exercises is an imagined dialogue, usually with a trusted moral authority, about the

circumstances and emotions surrounding the transgressive act: "[T]he intent is to create an atmosphere in which a forgiving and compassionate moral authority, sometimes through the voice of the patient and other times through the voice of the therapist, asks the service member or veteran to consider his or her condemning conclusions in light of the war experience itself and the stressors leading up to the event" (*Adaptive* 124). The dialogue resembles a "frank emotional confession" to a "secular moral authority" (128). The moral authority does not provide easy absolution but rather understanding, patience, and—ultimately—forgiveness.

The goal of the treatment is not a papering over of the transgressive act but rather an honest, thoroughgoing moral analysis that takes into account not only the evil of the event itself but the circumstances surrounding it and the other moral qualities of the morally injured person. Individuals are encouraged to move away from maladaptive, global evaluations like "*I am evil, I am worthless, I can never forgive myself*" (123) to more nuanced moral statements like "a complex self . . . contains the capacity for committing evil acts" and "worthwhile people do terrible things" (121). These dialogues often include (or are followed by) discussions of plans to make amends. Litz et al. write, "[T]here are ways to live that move toward decency and goodness, and that are helpful to other people. While it is impossible to 'fix' events in the past and, indeed, any focus on literal repair would likely ring hollow, there is the notion of making amends" (125). Such amends may include general good acts or tailored actions intended to address the specific wrongs either witnessed or done. Thus, one might support victims of similar wrongdoings or give to charities that might prevent such wrongdoings in the future (137). Litz et al. elaborate on a number of alternate versions of this part of adaptive disclosure that engage various iterations of moral injury, including betrayal and personal killing. We will return to adaptive disclosure in chapter 3 on MI and healing in Dostoevsky.

Now that we have created a sketch of the ways moral injury appears in the world, it is time to turn our attention to the ways it both shows up in and shapes literary text.

Notes

1. Shay acknowledges this difference in a 2012 article; for a new generation of moral injury researchers, he argues, "the violator is the self; in my definition the violator is a power-holder" ("Moral" 59). He nonetheless (at least grudgingly) validates the usefulness of Litz et al.'s update: "Moral injury . . . arises when a service member does something in war that violates their own ideals, ethics, or attachments. The diagnosis PTSD does not capture this. PTSD does a pretty good job of describing a kind of fear syndrome. Litz, et al. pointed out the central fact that PTSD, as officially defined, is rarely what wrecks veterans [*sic*] lives or crushes them to suicide. Moral injury as they have described it does both" (58).

2. Indeed, Litz et al. even allow for the possibility that moral injury may occur when the injured party is separated from the breach in both space and time. One may be injured when one visits the site of a wrong—or even when one simply "learns about" it.

3. Frankfurt et al. call them "potentially transgressive acts" (1951).

4. Currier et al.'s gathering of symptoms coincides roughly with my own: "[T]he symptoms of moral injury might include spiritual/existential problems (e.g., loss of spirituality or weakened religious faith, negative attributions towards G-d or higher power, lack of forgiveness and crisis in meaning), social issues (e.g. avoiding intimacy, anger/aggression towards others, reduced trust in other people and cultural contracts), inappropriate guilt and pervasive shame, substance abuse and other possible attempts at self-handicapping, suicide, and self-harm behaviors" ("Initial" 55).

5. Currier et al. also see a difference between the types of events that might trigger PTSD and MI diagnoses: "PMIEs can be distinguished from many Criterion A events. For instance, the criteria for PTSD does not explicitly reference acts of perpetration [American Psychiatric Association, 2013]. In addition, whereas Criterion A events are often characterized by a threat to life or physical integrity, MI events fundamentally entail a perceived violation of moral beliefs/values that lead an individual to appraise his or her experience as 'wrong'" ("Development" 476).

2

"My Sin Is Ever *before Me"*

MORAL INJURY AND LITERARY STYLE

Having defined and described moral injury in clinical terms, we may now turn our attention to literary depictions of it and its historical antecedents. In this chapter, my main project entails advancing a few theses regarding the ways in which moral injury sometimes inflects literary style. Indeed, MI shapes both individuals' conduct and their worldview—their works *and* their words. Thus, my central claim here is that literature engaging moral injury themes is often formally distinctive. Again, as I suggest in the introduction, my approach to these literatures is broadly "genealogical." I contend that in the ways they respond to evil, the characters discussed in the following chapters have family similarities to the veterans discussed in the previous chapter. And while I do not want to suggest that all of these characters are morally injured, I do argue that they respond to wrongdoing in ways that are both recognizable and predictable when viewed through the lens of MI. I also argue that we can see such responses in both contemporary and classic works.

The style of literature that engages moral injury themes can sometimes helpfully be characterized in terms of excess. Moral injury frequently makes evil feel superabundant, hyperpresent, and inescapable. These qualities are directly related to the nature of the affliction itself—which is similarly excessive. To review, the symptoms of MI are fourfold: anger/rage, social isolation, poor self-care, and the global negative evaluation of the self. The thread connecting these symptoms is a tendency toward *excess*. For the morally injured, anger threatens to slip into rage, withdrawal into total solitude, self-handicapping into parasuicidal or suicidal behavior. Likewise, those who suffer after doing wrong are increasingly unable to see their transgression as evil; rather, they begin to fear that *they* are evil—or that the world itself is irredeemably bad. The governing image here is of a malevolent superabundance, of a disease whose spread is unstoppable or an invasive species that has no natural competitors. The individual comes to see his or her sin as a cancer that may take over the self—or even the cosmos. One can hear evidence of the insidious creep of MI in the words of the VA psychologist Peter Yeomans. Speaking of his clients, he notes, "People try to make sense of what happened, but it often gets reduced to, 'It was my fault,' 'the world is dangerous,' or, in severe cases, 'I'm a monster'" (quoted in Wood, "'Good Person'"). MI makes it difficult to put an ethical error in context. Thus, some come to imagine their sin as ubiquitous and characterize their crime as having an extreme power to afflict.

No recent theorist is so frequently associated with the concept of excess than Georges Bataille, whose most systematic thinking on the theme appears in *The Accursed Share*. For Bataille, human life at both the individual and collective levels is characterized by oversupply—the overproduction of energy, goods, spectacles, money, and so on: "The living organism . . . receives more energy than is necessary for maintaining life. . . . [I]t must be spent, willingly or not, gloriously or catastrophically" (*Accursed* 21). The symptoms of MI can helpfully be understood in terms of such a "catastrophic" expenditure. We are exuberant, extravagant, hyperproductive. But MI gives a menacing cast to our natural energy, rendering it a force to be regretted and feared. Bataille predicts such negative emotions, arguing that when human exuberance erupts as violence (or, more specifically, war), it "characterizes this movement as something alien, hostile to human will" (38). Those with MI come to see their energies in just such a way, as both evil and uncontrollable.

Bataille argues that his theories of excess apply not only to economy and history but to art and literature as well; he writes, "Even what may be said of art, of literature, of poetry has an essential connection with the movement I study: that of excess energy" (*Accursed* 10). Thus, Bataille's thinking undergirds the way I approach the manifestation of moral injury themes in a variety of literatures. To wit, MI often warps the form of the works in which it appears, and those formal changes share a tendency toward excess.

If the governing trope of some literary depictions of moral injury is excess, one of its paradigmatic images is the tireless monologist who is compelled, somehow, to speak at length—perhaps even to try to say everything about the transgression in question. Moral injury feels like an oil spill in the soul, and those who suffer from it spray words like dispersants, scrambling to keep up with its spread. An overflow of speech—"saying everything"—is a manifestation of textual excess that Marcel Hénaff explores in his work on Sade. For Hénaff, Sade's writing pulses with an overwhelming urge to keep talking, keep describing. He imagines two forms of "saying everything": *trop*, to speak too much, and *tout*, to say it all. It is the latter that concerns us here: "The second connotation [of 'saying everything'] is that of *excess*. Here, saying 'everything' means the requirement to hide nothing, uncover everything" (55).[1] Saying and knowing are closely related here;

speech is a form of rational control, and the thing the morally injured person seeks to know again is the self. MI renders the psyche alien, and saying everything is an effort to relearn the contours of a self that suddenly feels terrifyingly like an other. In certain circumstances, Hénaff notes, "'Saying everything,' considered as the ambition to 'tell all,' is . . . the business of paranoia" (62). Such is the case with the logorrhea of MI; if we cannot say (or know) everything about this newly foreign self, our imaginations wander to dark places. In this vein, Hénaff quotes Bataille: "The crime is concealed, and what is most terrifying is what escapes us. We are obliged, in the night it offers our fear, to imagine the worst" (Hénaff 76). To avoid obsessing about the worst, the morally injured try to speak the all in hopes of driving out the unknown. They seek

> the destruction of the secret's last hideout, of the last possibility for prohibition. Everything must be said so that the ineffable will be left no toehold. Where excess is concerned, so long as what comes into play has not been said, *everything* has not yet been said; indeed, *nothing at all* has been said, in keeping with the principle that we'll know nothing unless we acquaint ourselves with everything. (72)

And indeed, exhausted speakers driven by this impossible urge to acquaint themselves with everything often fill the pages of literature that engages MI themes.

A number of characters suffice to establish this pattern. Leslie Marmon Silko's poignant, wrenching novel *Ceremony* tells the story of the Laguna Pueblo veteran Tayo as he struggles with the fallout of his participation in World War II. Perhaps the most damaging of his experiences occurs when his commanding officer orders his company to execute a group of Japanese POWs.

As shots are fired, Tayo swears that he sees the face of his Uncle Josiah among the crowd of falling soldiers. Telling other veterans of his experience years later, Tayo is barely able to contain the narrative, which jostles about inside him with almost physical force: "He could feel the words coming out faster and faster, the momentum building inside him like the words were all going to explode and he wanted to finish before it happened" (42). We see an analogous "momentum"—this time literally etched in stone—in Toni Morrison's *Beloved*. In that book, the protagonist Sethe, after killing her daughter Beloved, ponders the inscription on her child's tombstone. Though it will ultimately be just one word long—her daughter's name—she dreams that it might be much longer, encompassing all the words of the funeral sermon and maybe more: "[S]he could have had the whole thing, every word she heard the preacher say at the funeral (and all there was to say, surely) engraved on her baby's headstone" (5). The gnomic phrase "all there was to say" reads two ways: either the sermon somehow captures everything that needs to be said about Beloved's death, or, more comprehensively, all the words in the world are necessary to communicate the gravity of the moment, the depth of Sethe's anguish, the ache of the baby's absence.

Older texts feature similar patterns. Tancred not only bursts with words; he sees the repeated telling of his tale as punishment for his sin:

> So I shall live to tell my wretched tale
> for my life merits nothing more than pain—
> wretched example of unhappy love—
> for the immense crime it is guilty of. (Tasso 246)

Here, dramatically, life equals pain, and the pain springs from the story of the misdeed Tancred feels compelled to tell about. These comments come in the immediate aftermath of Clorinda's death. Yet even later, when his conscience has cooled, he remains pressed to continue verbalizing his pain, so that even when "his inner grief grew cooler in offense," he cannot "prevent a sigh / or his tongue giving rein to his laments" (248). In between these two quotations, Tasso likens Tancred's words to blood flowing from a wound that will not heal; as he lies abed, struggling to survive the cuts that nearly kill him, blood and words flow interchangeably from his body:

> And he cuts short
> His words—a desperate longing moves him now,
> Longing to die—he tears apart
> His bandages, rips wide his wounds, lets flow
> A river of blood from his body freshly hurt,
> And would have killed himself had not great pain
> Preserved his life and made him faint again. (247)

His physical wounds, it seems, are like his moral wounds, and both stubbornly refuse to be staunched.

Coleridge's ancient mariner is similarly compelled to tell and retell the tale of his wrongs. He sins, of course, in killing the albatross, but this small error leads to the torturously slow starvation of all his crewmates in the doldrums that follow. The only survivor, the ancient mariner, witnesses each man's death, knowing he is responsible for them all. But rather than bury what must be a harrowing narrative, he feels compelled to tell and retell it in detail. Shortly after his miraculous return to land, the mariner speaks of a "woful agony / Which forced me to begin my tale" (137; lines 580–81). He continues, explaining the compulsion that returns him frequently to his story:

> Since then, at an uncertain hour,
> That agony returns:

And till my ghastly tale is told,
This heart within me burns.

I pass, like night, from land to land;
I have strange power of speech;
That moment that his face I see,
I know the man that must hear me:
To him my tale I teach. (137; lines 583–90)

Here, the mariner intimates that Coleridge's poem is just one iteration of a narrative circle that turns endlessly.[2] And that the narrative returns at "uncertain" times indicates that it rolls on out of his control. Another example is the prince-king Yudhisthira from the Indian epic *Mahabharata*, which recounts the story of the internecine war between the Pandavas and the Kauravas. In the wake of his involvement in a battle that takes the lives of family members, Yudhisthira is overcome by a sense of shame that gnaws long after his family and friends have moved on. Frequently throughout books 11 through 14 of the *Mahabharata*, Yudhisthira launches into monologues describing his persistent anguish, repeatedly threatening to give up his throne and retire forever to the wilderness. Again, a compulsion to speak marks the prince's pain.

Yet the effects of MI on literary style are not merely quantitative; or, more succinctly, MI does not merely produce lots of text. Moral injury themes may alter other elements of style, from diction to imagery to metaphor. Bataille says something similar in a brief but packed reading of the unpublished outline of a play conceived by Baudelaire. In it, a sawyer spurned by his wife arranges to meet her again for a nighttime walk, during which he kills his love by steering her into a hidden well. Bataille argues that this sin reshapes the text's form "by way of a change of key. . . . It is deformed and changes" (*Literature* 50). The effects of this key change push the language toward the "rejection of limitation"—toward excess (50). In literature that engages MI themes, this key change often manifests in three primary tropes: hyperbole, sublimity, and what I will call "signs of solitude." Let me address them in that order.

We begin with hyperbole—with the exaggerations that fill the language of morally injured individuals. As a real-life example, we can turn to the language of a military chaplain writing from Afghanistan in 2013. In describing his suffering, he reflects on the damage done by drones both in and outside that conflict:

> One of the primary causes of my moral anguish—five months living under drones at Kandahar Airfield I thought—I don't have thoughts of harming someone else, but I know about the Commander-in-Chief really—and he has this kill list . . . and *a whole fleet of armed drones* to execute *on demand all over the world.* . . . War hurts, and the moral pain can be the most excruciating wound of war—the moral pain of knowing I helped cause the innocent to suffer, like when a hell-fire missile launched remotely from an unmanned drone rips through the *most intimate spaces* of living rooms and the *most sacred grounds* of schools. (quoted in Tick 84; emphasis mine)

The chaplain is psychologically wounded by the murders he perceives himself as having abetted. Yet when he speaks of the victims of the drone strikes—and of the drones themselves—he does so hyperbolically. Of course, drones likely feel as if they are omnipresent, but in truth the US has deployed them in relatively few areas. Yet the chaplain exaggerates both their reach and their efficacy; they are "on demand all over the world." And when they strike, it is as if they are designed to do the most objectionable harm, penetrating the "most intimate spaces" and the "most sacred grounds." Drone damage is horrific, but the chaplain renders the violence it does unbearable. We see similar patterns of exaggeration in literary depictions of moral injury.

Hyperbole's connection to excess might seem apparent, but both Bataille and Christopher Johnson clarify the links between the two terms. Writing of Sade's language, Bataille suggests that the author's hyperbole marks moments when "excess can no longer be gauged" (*Literature* 119). And in Johnson's book on the device, he writes, "Excess corresponds to the extraordinary idea or emotional effect (*affectus*) produced, while hyperbole is the linguistic means to achieve this" (8).[3] Accordingly, insofar as writing featuring MI themes often tries to capture "extraordinary emotional effects," it features a brand of hyperbole that suggests that language is struggling to hold in the enormity of the individual's experience of sin. For Johnson, such a struggle is constitutive of hyperbole as a trope: "The hyperbolist perceives an extraordinary, outrageous, ridiculous, or ineffable *res* (thing, event, feeling, idea), while his or her *verba* (words, speech, language) strain discursive limits, analogical frameworks, and literary and rhetorical conventions, to represent that *res*" (2). In literature that engages MI themes, the crime is the *res* that hyperbolic *verba* strain to inscribe.[4] Thus, pain can be fathomless, criminals irredeemable, emptiness total, and judgments universal. Or as Edgar says in Shakespeare's *King Lear*, "And worse I may be yet. The worst is not / So long as we can say, 'This is the worst'" (87; IV, i, 29–30). Authors often use the device to show how sin feels excessively severe, expansive, long, or effective.

To the first, characters often describe their crimes as singularly horrible. Macbeth, for instance, imagines that his murders—of Duncan, Banquo, and Macduff's family—have somehow initiated a new form of homicide that is qualitatively more damaging than previous versions:

> [M]urders have been perform'd
> Too terrible for the ear: the times have been,
> That, when the brains were out, the man would die,
> And there an end; but now they rise again,
> With twenty mortal murders on their crowns,
> And push us from our stools: this is more strange
> Than such a murder is. (111; III, iv, 78–84)

Here we have something like a calculus of destruction: Macbeth sees his misdeeds as multiplicatively powerful, spawning exponentially more death. Previous murders, he argues, were "too terrible"; his, however, push even further beyond the pale.

In similar fashion, Sartre's war criminal Franz, in *The Condemned of Altona*, imagines himself as helping perpetrate the most heinous crime ever: "The razed towns, the smashed machines, the looted industry, the steep rise in unemployment and tuberculosis, and the sharp fall in the birth rate. Nothing escapes me. My sister copies out all the statistics. They are all filed in this drawer. The finest murder in history" (85). Notice first that Franz, like Macbeth, wants some sort of computational analysis of his crimes; "statistics" help him reach a quantitative measure of their effects. These extreme crimes, then, may leave extreme marks on the memory of those who commit or experience them. John Wade, the main character of Tim O'Brien's *In the Lake of the Woods*, is a Vietnam veteran who is present at the massacre at Thuan Yen—a thinly veiled My Lai. Wade describes the events of Thuan Yen as "pure wrongness" (105) and says later, "This was sin" (107). Unfortunately, from Wade's perspective, this sin etches itself indelibly and ineradicably onto his mind: he "would remember Thuan Yen the way chemical nightmares are remembered, impossible combinations, impossible events, and over time the impossibility itself would become *the richest and deepest and most profound memory"* (109; emphasis mine). And this memory, then, pursues Wade relentlessly.

Given that these sins feel so gigantically bad, characters often describe them as stretching out over space and through time. Macbeth sees his crimes as a sea of blood unfolding in all directions: "I am in blood / Stepp'd in so far that, should I wade no more, / Returning were as tedious as go o'er" (113; III, iv, 137–39). In similar fashion, Franz imagines (delusionally) walking home from Russia after the war, stumbling through Germany and seeing signs reading "YOU ARE GUILTY" spotting the landscape. "They've put them *everywhere*," he mutters (139; emphasis mine). Likewise, the furies imagine that Orestes's crime in killing his mother is so atrocious that it will pursue him to the ends of the earth:

> Nevertheless keep racing on and never yield.
> Deep in the endless heartland they will drive you,
> Striding horizons, feet pounding the earth for ever,
> On, on over seas and cities swept by tides!
> Never surrender, never brood on the labour. (Aeschylus 234)[5]

The irony here is that while Orestes may "brood" on his act, the furies will have no time to do so, busy as they are chasing him.

Implicit in all of these images is the skewed notion of an evil that has come to infect the whole world, that has shaped all existence to its dark purposes. As mentioned previously, this suspicion is one of the key markers of moral injury. In *Ceremony*, the elder Betonie counsels Tayo against seeing the world as wholly disfigured by the presence of evil, which the novel frequently refers to as "witchery." He says, "Some people act like witchery is responsible for everything that happens, when actually witchery only manipulates a small portion" (130). Yet Tayo often forgets Betonie's advice, exaggerating witchery's reach and influence: "There was no end to it; it knew no boundaries; and he had arrived at the point of convergence where the fate of all living things, and even the earth, had been laid" (246). Here, the witchery to which Tayo's perceived transgressions connect him reaches not only to the ends of the earth but to the beginning of the universe.

Last, hyperbole allows individuals to describe their crimes as nearly infinite in their ramifications; the effects ripple out endlessly. The narrator of Tasso's tale warns Tancred before his battle with Clorinda, "If you live your eyes shall pay, / for every drop of blood of hers you spill, / a sea of grief" (242). The relationship between blood and tears—or sin and pain—is exponential, and Tancred will be tormented by his crime to the nth degree. In similar fashion, Macbeth sees the effects of his crime unspool both geographically and temporally—or perhaps generationally. He is plagued by the thought that his actions will lead to an endless dynasty for Banquo's line:

> What, will the line stretch out to the crack of doom?
> Another yet! A seventh! I'll see no more:
> And yet the eighth appears, who bears a glass
> Which shows me many more; and some I see
> That two-fold balls and treble scepters carry:
> Horrible sight! (121; IV, i, 117–22)

Will the line stretch to the crack of doom? No. Yet moral injury makes Macbeth feel as if it will, and hyperbole allows him to express that sensation.

The effects of moral injury in literature are not apparent only in the authors' choice of literary devices. They also color imagery. As moral injury slowly dims the vision of those who suffer it, the world they see begins to take on a more and more menacing cast.

It seems as if nature itself turns on the person with MI. Take, as an example, the story David Wood tells of Darren Doss, a veteran of the war in Afghanistan. One day, members of Doss's unit shoot and kill a man acting suspiciously in a nearby field. The man is forgotten until a few days later, when a young boy convinces Doss and some other marines to go out with him to see the man's corpse. The dead man, it turns out, is the boy's father; he had been "acting suspiciously" because he was deaf and mute—and hence couldn't respond to warning shots. The rotting body had been ravaged by dogs (*What* 140). This fact has a piercing effect on Doss, whose own father long struggled with a variety of health problems. After returning home from Afghanistan, Doss has nightmares that bring him back to that day in the farmer's field; in these dreams, "he is back in Afghanistan, going out into that field with Canty and the Afghan boy, and they find the corpse, but instead of the Afghan man who'd been dead for days, it's his father, and his father's face is partially eaten away . . . by dogs" (141). In the figure of these demonic dogs, the natural world becomes terrifying.

To capture the menace of nature that sometimes afflicts those who suffer from moral injury, authors writing about it often resort to something like the Romantic sublime. Hurricanes bear down, animal hordes threaten, rising tides overwhelm, and deserts stretch to the horizon. And yet when the sublime appears, it is a more expansive category than, say, Burke's narrower version of the term. To elaborate, we might turn to Fredric Jameson's discussion of sublimity. In "Pleasure: A Political Issue," Jameson writes of the sublime in terms of an "apprehension through a given aesthetic object of what in its awesome magnitude shrinks, threatens, diminishes, rebukes individual human life" (72). Elsewhere, he explains the sublime as "an experience bordering on terror, the fitful glimpse, in astonishment, stupor and awe, of what was so enormous as to crush human life altogether" ("Postmodernism" 77).[6] So far so good. But we consult Jameson rather than Burke— or Burke via Jameson—because Jameson applies the sublime to a wider variety of objects. For Burke, the sublime is found primarily in God and nature. For Jameson, by contrast, we may find the sublime almost anywhere—in the "impossible totality of the contemporary world system" and (more abstractly) in that "other reality of economic and social institutions" (78). Jameson's sublime, then, is helpful for understanding the ways afflicted individuals might view the world in its entirety as awe-ful or terrifying.[7]

As mentioned in the previous chapter, the morally injured often seek to isolate themselves. Thus Yudhisthira threatens to retire from house and throne and take up the life of a desert ascetic after the war that claims the lives of his kinsmen. Others, however, wander alone into a wilderness that is sublimely threatening. For instance, after killing Clorinda, Tancred bravely (or foolhardily) takes on the task of exploring a cursed forest whose wood his army needs to build the siege works necessary to continue their attack on Jerusalem. Tasso describes the wood in chilling terms:

> But after sunset in this forest all
> is smoke and horror and the depths of night,
> as deep a darkness as the black of hell,
> that fills the heart with fear, and robs the sight.
> Never the shepherd, never the cowherd will
> lead herd or flock to feed in that ill light,
> and the wary traveler, unless he's lost his way,
> points it out as he passes far away. (253)

This forest is a natural scene recast as a hellscape—a smoky, horrible, dark, blinding place that, it seems, threatens to swallow the lost. That Tancred finds there a bleeding tree that traps the soul of his dead love only drives the point home.

Lear faces a similarly ominous countryside as he flees into the heath after realizing the bitter deserts of his betrayal of Cordelia. And in the tempest that batters him, we find no better example of moral injury's sublime. Lear cries,

> Blow, wind, and crack your cheeks! Rage, blow,
> You cataracts and hurricanoes, spout
> Till you have drenched our steeples, drowned the cocks!
> You sulph'rous and thought-executing fires,
> Vaunt-couriers of oak-cleaving thunderbolts,
> Singe my white head. And thou all-shaking thunder,
> Strike flat the thick rotundity o'th'world,
> Crack nature's moulds, all germens spill at once
> That makes ingrateful man. (63–64; III, ii, 1–9)

What is more surprising than the unnatural power of the "cataracts," perhaps, is the fact that Lear himself discerns a relationship between the careering storm and the moral failings of those caught in its path. He calls on the gods of vengeance and justice to let the gale flush out sinners and reveal their crimes:

> Let the great gods,
> That keep this dreadful pudder o'er our heads,
> Find out their enemies now. Tremble, thou wretch,
> That hast within thee undivulged crimes
> Unwhipped of justice. Hide thee, thou bloody hand,
> Thou perjured and thou simular of virtue
> That art incestuous. (65; III, ii, 49–55)

This strange storm, it seems, has uncanny moral power; it lays bare hypocrisy and exposes counterfeit goodness. Of course, this speech ends with one of Lear's most famous lines: "I am a

man / More sinned against than sinning" (65; III, ii, 49–59). And
yet the fact that Lear acknowledges his own wrongs in its last two
words indicates that he too is being "whipped of justice" by the
stiff blast.

But perhaps the sublimity of nature is even more terrifying
when we expect something else, something better. Such is the case
in *Beloved*, when the terrors of the world are amplified by our expectations that it should instead be tender and beautiful. Sethe
says as much of Sweet Home, the bucolic plantation whose graces
are marred by the crimes committed there. And as Sethe notes, its
natural splendor set its evils in stark relief:

> [S]uddenly there was Sweet Home rolling, rolling, rolling out be-
> fore her eyes, and although there was not a leaf on that farm that
> did not make her want to scream, it rolled itself out before her in
> shameless beauty. It never looked as terrible as it was and it made
> her wonder if hell was a pretty place too. Fire and brimstone all
> right, but hidden in lacy gloves. Boys hanging from the most beau-
> tiful sycamores in the world. (6)

The implication here is that human sin spoils the loveliness and
harmony of nature and turns a heaven into an inferno. Something similar happens in Jesmyn Ward's 2017 novel, *Sing, Unburied, Sing*. In it, a young African American woman, Leonie, is
rocked first by the murder of her brother, Given, by white class-
mates and then by a subsequent cover-up of that crime by local
authorities. After witnessing both of these transgressions, Leonie
falls into a tailspin whose sequelae include both drug abuse and
neglect of her children. This sequence of events seemingly poisons the world. When she was young, Leonie's mother taught
her how to turn roots, berries, and other natural products into
medicines and balms. Her mother's healing craft draws on a

benevolent natural world that helps humans both survive and thrive. But in the novel's present, that world is gone, leaving behind less hospitable landscapes that withhold their gifts. Accordingly, when Leonie tries to find plants she might use to ease her own daughter's sickness, they are nowhere to be found: "If the world were a right place, a place for the living . . . I'd be able to find wild strawberries. That's what Mama would look for if she couldn't find milkweed. . . . But the world ain't that place. Ain't no wild strawberries at the side of the road" (105).

Yet moral injury's sublime infects not only nature but other parts of the cosmos. Here, Jameson's broader characterization of the term becomes helpful. Let us turn our attention once more to *The Condemned of Altona*. For the protagonist in that play, human (or superhuman?) technology begins to take on an ominous cast. For instance, at one point the addled Franz imagines human ingenuity as bending toward an explosive apocalypse: "The explosion of the planet is on the agenda, and the scientists have their finger on the button. Goodbye!" (118) Yet a less obvious example of the Jamesonian sublime is actually more telling. Among the iterations of the sublime that intrigues Jameson is what he calls the "technological sublime." McAvan explains the phenomenon, in which "the ungraspable nature of electronic communications in global late capitalism produces an awe akin to earlier romantic notions of the sublime" (405). Franz's delusions produce a telling example of the technological sublime in the invisible recording membrane built and deployed by the crab race: "Imagine a black window. Finer than ether. Ultra-sensitive. It records the slightest breath. The slightest breath. All history is engraved on it, from the beginning of time up to this snap of my fingers. . . . We're under observation all the time" (63–64). What a fearsome prospect; in such a strange alternate universe, those suffering the burden of their own shame face the possibility that their acts will be forever inscribed in the very fabric of history. Yet all of these invocations of sublimity—in landscape, weather, fauna, and technology—make sense given the outlook of those who suffer moral injury: an ominous, threatening world is a fit place for ominous, threatening people.

There is often a paradoxical quality to the sense of demoralization that accompanies moral injury. As the individual's sense of his or her own evil grows, the inescapability of the corrupted self becomes more apparent—and perhaps even more darkly attractive. Put differently, in the wake of wrongdoing, the soul is a black hole whose gravitational force only grows. As Bataille says in *Literature and Evil*, some of those who do wrong come to understand "the abyss which man is for himself" (93). After killing Clorinda, Tancred has just such an abyssal self, a soul that vexes, maddens, and yet is inescapably present. Tancred is a man trapped with—and vexed by—a self that is becoming other. He cries, "I will fear even myself, and try to hide, / But I will always have me at my side" (Tasso 246).

We hear echoes of Tancred's voice in the words of Air Force colonel Erik Goepner, who isolates himself after service in a war effort he comes to understand as unethical. Sherman writes,

> The corrosive environment and futility of the operations hit [Goepner] personally: "Anyone who comes close to that environment is going to come away maybe not ruined but tarnished, dirtied, sullied. . . . I'm fairly introverted anyway—but I became *hugely* introverted. I had a very strong desire to disengage from most everything. . . . [I]n terms of my wife, in particular, I was *very disengaging*. . . . [M]y response was instead of ever getting angry or yelling at anybody, I just disengaged. I didn't want to spend time with them, I'd read a book, I'd do some writing or something like

that. . . . I'd say I now have a higher need for privacy and alone-
time than I used to." (27)

As Goepner reflects on his time at war, he sees himself as blem-
ished and then seeks to be alone. Yet his desire to distance himself
from others has subtle effects on the way he speaks. First, as he
talks about his introversion, he relies frequently on first-person
pronouns; we see his self-as-grammatical-subject alone more
often. His choice of imagery similarly reflects his withdrawal. Notice the word he uses to explain his estrangement from his wife:
"disengaging." This participle evokes not only his solitude but the
beginning of his now-crumbling marriage, the engagement. As his
relationship with his partner falls apart, this reversal of marital
images—from engagement to disengagement—serves to emphasize
the pain caused by their separation. In sum, we can see Goepner's
isolation not only in his message, but in his diction and imagery.

I call these two stylistic effects "signs of solitude," adapting a
phrase from Jeff Nunokawa. In an excellent essay on George Eliot's
Adam Bede, Nunokawa writes of "signs of . . . [separation]" in that
novel that either reflect or predict characters' actual separations
from one another. For instance, as Adam realizes his alienation
from Hetty and his friend Arthur Donnithorne, we see images of
separation amass in the text. As Adam walks through the wood,
Nunokawa writes, he sees a "'beech'—so *close in sound to breech*—
the tree he *singles out* from the forest, '*at a turning in the road*,' not
'two trees welded together, but *only one*'" (836; emphasis mine).
Along with these visual symbols of separation, Nunokawa also
tracks a "drift from plural to singular" in the number of the text's
nouns that further emphasizes Adam's split from his friends (836).
I argue that in literature, in a similar way, both diction and imagery reflect the morally injured person's isolation.

Two telling examples effectively demonstrate characters' over-reliance on the first person. The first comes from *Adam Bede*. Near the end of the novel, Dinah visits Hetty in jail, where the latter awaits her trial for infanticide. After a period of tortured silence, Dinah extracts Hetty's confession, which gushes forth with force. In that confession, which runs to roughly 1,700 words, Eliot has Hetty use the first-person "I" no fewer than 150 times. A brief excerpt drives the point home:

> But I thought perhaps it wouldn't die—there might somebody find it. I didn't kill it—I didn't kill it myself. I put it down there and covered it up, and when I came back it was gone. . . . It was because I was so very miserable, Dinah. . . . I didn't know where to go . . . and I tried to kill myself before, and I couldn't. Oh, I tried so to drown myself in the pool, and I couldn't. I went to Windsor—I ran away—did you know? I went to find him, as he might take care of me; and he was gone; and then I didn't know what to do. I daredn't go back home again—I couldn't bear it. (467)

The pattern continues unabated throughout the rest of the passage and serves only to reinforce the sense that Hetty is sinking in the "dark gulf" that is her self.

In *Sing, Unburied, Sing*, Leonie is also trapped in a sort of "gulf" after the murder of her brother, and the formal effects of her isolation are similar. After Given is killed, Leonie tries to throw herself back into social life, but even when she is around others, she remains separated from her surroundings. Here is one notable example, where the ghost of her brother visits her at a party. As she describes the evening, the "I"s once again pile up:

> I ground my gums sore staring at Given. I ate him with my eyes. He tried to talk to me but I couldn't hear him, and he just got more and more frustrated. He sat on the table in front of me, right on

the mirror with the coke on it. I couldn't put my face in it again without putting it in his lap, so we sat there staring at each other, me trying not to react so I wouldn't look crazy to my friends, who were singing along to country music, kissing sloppily in corners like teenagers, walking in zigzags with their arms linked out into the dark. Given looked at me like he did when we were little and I broke the new fishing pole Pop got him: murderous. When I came down, I almost ran out to my car. I was shaking so hard, I could hardly put my key in the ignition. Given climbed in next to me, sat in the passenger seat, and turned and looked at me with a face of stone. *I quit*, I said. *I swear I won't do it no more.* (52)

The first-person pronouns come hard and fast in the last line, four in seven words as she tries to banish her brother's specter and re-join the community of the living.

We also see signs of solitude in the images authors use to de-scribe morally injured individuals. Returning once more to Tasso, images of solitude both anticipate and echo Tancred's own with-drawal. First, Tancred is able to kill Clorinda mainly because she is separated from the rest of her army; alone, she is easier prey, and her allies lament the fact that she is vulnerable: "[S]hut out alone is she" (240). An even more fully developed such sign is the tree in which Clorinda's soul is trapped after her death. As Tancred unwittingly stumbles upon it in the cursed wood, it is dramatically set apart from the rest of the blasted forest:

> At last he found a wide and open space
> formed like an amphitheater, and free
> of any vegetation save one proud
> towering pyramid of a cypress tree
> in the dead center. (260)

That the space is not merely "open" but "like an amphitheater" em-phasizes the fact that the tree is not only isolated but thoroughly exposed. And just as Clorinda is alone in her death and her terrifying afterlife, so too is Tancred radically cut off from community and aid by his suffering.

Coleridge's "Rime" also features many images that both reflect and emphasize the speaker's solitude. "Alone, alone, all, all alone, / Alone on a wide, wide sea" (121; lines 233–34), he says of his own state, and many other things in the poem are similarly alone. The wedding guest compelled to hear the mariner's tale is split off from his companions at the outset: "[H]e stoppeth one of three" (109; line 2). That the wedding ceremony goes on even as the auditor listens serves to emphasize his separation from his mates:

> The bride hath paced into the hall,
> Red as a rose is she;
> Nodding their heads before her goes
> The merry minstrelsy (111; lines 33–36).

Later in the poem, when the mariner tells the story of his shipmates' demise, he suggests that they do not perish en masse, but "one by one," each separated from the other in the moment of his passing:

> *One after one*, by the star-dogg'd Moon,
> To quick for groan or sigh,
> Each turn'd his face with a ghastly pang,
> And cursed me with his eye.
>
> Four times fifty living men
> (And I heard nor sigh nor groan),
> With heavy thump, a lifeless lump,
> They dropp'd down *one by one*. (120; lines 213–20; emphasis mine)

That each of these two hundred aims a piercing gaze at the mariner—again, "one by one"—turns the catastrophe into a slow-rolling, macabre spectacle.

After they die, other, less obvious signs of solitude pop up throughout the piece. Later, the mariner describes the evil that emanates from the corpses' eyes as worse than "an orphan's curse" (122; line 258). When the reanimated corpse of one of the ship-mates rises to help the mariner steer the ship home, the two pull "at one rope" (126; line 344). And as the mariner moves to re-join the community of humans near the poem's end, images of company and separation—plural and singular—combine. As their trials near completion, the corpses come together in song, sometimes together and sometimes alone: "Slow the sounds came back again, / Now mix'd, now one by one" (126; lines 357–58). In a similar aural image a few lines later, the mariner hears the call of the skylark, first in chorus, then as a solo: "And now 'twas like all instruments, / Now like a lonely flute" (127; lines 364–65). It is as if Coleridge is tempting the mariner with the succor of society. Yet as the poem winds down, he reveals that temptation as hollow, and more signs of solitude emphasize the mariner's continuing isolation—and his moral injury. Even after the alba-tross's curse is broken, the mariner continues on "like one that on a *lonesome* road / Doth walk in fear and dread" (131; lines 447–48; emphasis mine). And who is one of the figures to find the mariner when he returns to land but a holy hermit, living in solitude by the water's edge.

We see a similar proliferation of signs of solitude at the end of *In the Lake of the Woods*. John Wade, a suspect in his wife's disappear-ance, still tormented by his wartime past, sets off alone on a small fishing boat into the lake of the book's title, eventually to disappear into the winter wilderness. As he does, the narrative brims with markers of his loneliness. The Lake of the Woods takes up most of what is called the Northwest Angle, a single bump in the US-Canadian border and the only piece of the contiguous United States to push above the 49th parallel: "[S]tranded by a mapmaker's error, the Angle represents the northernmost point in the lower 48 states, a remote spit of woods and water surrounded on three sides by Canada" (286). The Angle is a lonely, unique cartographical error, a "geographical orphan," O'Brien writes (286). As he describes it, other signs crop up. "A lone hawk circles in hunt" (286); "A single tar road runs through deep forest to the small community of Angle Inlet" (287). And eventually, these signs slip into solipsism, as "in the deep unbroken solitude, age to age, Lake of the Woods gazes back on itself like a great liquid eye" (286–87).

Having identified some of the tropes that frequently shape literature engaging moral injury and its antecedents, we may now turn our attention to some more telling examples of works that contain them. The next three chapters are ordered chronologically, and each focuses on a different type of moral injury. These flavors become more nuanced as we go. In *Crime and Punishment*, Raskolnikov's pain is the straightforward result of an act of commission: a brutal double murder. In the next, Camus's protagonist Clamence suffers primarily as the result of an act of omission: his failure to stop a suicide. In the third of these chapters, Kevin Powers's soldier-heroes are morally injured committing, failing to stop, and witnessing bad acts, but that pain is accentuated by stateside civilians' ignorance of them—indeed, by the fact that the latter are *not* morally injured. Let's begin.

Notes

1. In *Literature and Evil*, Bataille finds an example of "saying everything" in the diaries of Kafka. "What is this excess?" the author writes. "How everything can be said; how, for every idea that comes to mind, even for the strangest ideas, a great fire waits for them to disappear and resurrect" (162).

2. On returning from the camps, Primo Levi sees himself in just these terms, as compelled to speak ad nauseam about the evils he witnesses: "You remember

the scene: the Ancient Mariner accosts the wedding guests, who are thinking of the wedding and not paying attention to him, and he forces them to listen to his tale. Well, when I first returned from the concentration camp I did just that. I felt an unrestrainable need to tell my story to anyone and everyone! . . . Every situation was an occasion to tell my story to anyone and everyone: to tell it to the factory director as well as to the worker, even if they had other things to do. I was reduced to the state of the Ancient Mariner. Then I began to write on my typewriter at night. . . . Every night I would write, and this was considered even crazier" (quoted in Agamben 16).

3. Johnson contends that hyperbole is something more than a simple literary device for baroque artists: "Baroque hyperbole is more than a figure of style: it is a mode of thought, a way of being. Even when it takes the seemingly transparent form of an invidious comparison, we discover that to compare invidiously can be to place inordinate, potentially untenable weight on the writer's subjectivity. The hyperbolist measures the tension between the ideal and the real, the distance between the word and the world" (5).

4. Again, Johnson is helpful on this point: "With hyperbole the speaker again suggests that language is poorly suited to represent the *res*, but now he opts for too much, exaggerated, or conceptually audacious speech" (9).

5. Admittedly, a reading of the *Eumenides* does not bear out the claim that Orestes suffers from moral injury. Indeed, he seems quite able to situate the murder of his Clytemnestra in a particular place and time—and to provide a plausible, defensible motive for his acts.

6. Though they do not significantly affect my argument, Helmling points out subtle differences between Jameson's treatment of the sublime in these two texts: "In 'Pleasure,' 'the sublime' functions to bring apparently divergent and conflicting motifs—'fear' and 'jouissance,' preeminently—to a concentrated focus; it disciplines a variety of impulses or affects to a single effect. In 'Postmodernism,' by contrast, it functions to loosen or even reverse this inexorable 'winner loses logic.' If the earlier essay inflects 'jouissance' with historical terror, the later enables the transformation of 'fear' or 'shock' back into 'joyous intensities'" (6).

7. To drive the point home, we may also return once more to Bataille. Again reflecting on Sade in *Literature and Evil*, Bataille writes that "the language of *Les Cent Vingt Journees de Sodome* is that of a universe which degrades gradually and systematically, which tortures and destroys the totality of the beings which it presents" (122). Such is the cosmos as viewed through the eyes of the afflicted perpetrator; it eternally threatens and seems to endanger all its inhabitants.

3

Moral Injury and Moral Repair in Crime and Punishment

Why does Raskolnikov kill? For many readers of Dostoevsky's best-known work, *Crime and Punishment*, this is the crucial question. In his magisterial biography of the author, Joseph Frank frames the approach this question entails very effectively. Dostoevsky, Frank writes, "is focused on the solution of an enigma: the mystery of Raskolnikov's motivation. For Raskolnikov himself, as it turns out, discovers that he does not understand *why* he killed" (102). Frank goes on to argue that our analysis of this enigma turns *Crime and Punishment* into a sort of metamystery: "The usual quest for the murderer in the detective story plot," he writes, "is transferred to the character himself; it is now Raskolnikov who searches for *his own* motivation" (102). Indeed, even to the novel's last pages, the killer's reasons remain unclear, both to himself and to the reader. Does he murder for money, to relieve his own oppressive penury? Or does he do so to help his sister and mother avoid a similar fate? Does he kill to prove that he is a "Napoleon"—that he can "step over" moral laws meant only for lesser people? Or does he kill for utilitarian reasons, doing a small evil in pursuit of a greater good? Indeed, all of these theories seem persuasive at discrete points in the novel, and none wins out in its final pages.

However, as Derek Allan points out in a 2016 article, there is a second major question that animates scholars interested in *Crime and Punishment*: what is the cause behind—and the nature of—Raskolnikov's postmurder psychological breakdown? (133) Answers to this question are fewer and farther between, at least in recent years, perhaps in part because of Bakhtin's suggestion in his decisive *Problems of Dostoevsky's Poetics* that "Dostoevsky did not consider himself a psychologist in any sense of the term" (62).[1] The Russian theorist's claims notwithstanding, some of the earliest, most incisive readings of Dostoevsky are "psychological." Prime among these is a book by the nineteenth-century clinician Vladimir Fedorovich Chizh, who sees Dostoevsky "as a great intuitive observer and master at portraying abnormal psychic phenomena" (quoted in Rice 201) and whose book enumerates the many examples of this "mastery" evident in the novels. James L. Rice finds Chizh's readings persuasive, in no small part because Dostoevsky "unquestionably had frequent recourse to the latest medical literature . . . especially works dealing with diseases of the brain, the nervous system, and the psyche" (109). Yuri Corrigan agrees, contending that we should "approach Dostoevskii first and foremost not as an ideologue but as a psychologist" (227). In this chapter, I hope to contribute to this effort with an analysis of moral injury themes in *Crime and Punishment*.

Of course, the "psychological Dostoevsky" in the novel has long been hiding in plain sight. In an oft-quoted letter to his publisher, Katkov, in which he pitches an early version of the book, the author describes it as a "psychological account of a crime" and describes the postmurder plot as the "entire psychological process of crime [unfolding] itself" (Frank and Goldstein 221, 222). Dostoevsky shares these concerns with his main character, and Raskolnikov describes his own writing—in an article written during his student years—as an examination of the "psychological state of the criminal throughout the course of the crime" (258). This article has drawn the attention of many critics, especially those who see Raskolnikov as a sort of intellectual killer—or, in Mochulsky's memorable turn of phrase, a "theoretician murderer" (293). Those who find this interpretation persuasive mine the article's argument that certain crimes might be acceptable for certain people at certain times. The novel's police inspector, Porfiry, finds such suggestions both disturbing and ultimately incriminating, as they apparently provide a rationalization for heinous acts. These are eye-catching suggestions, but their flash and sparkle tend to distract readers from another of Raskolnikov's central ideas in the essay: that crime makes a perpetrator sick. As Porfiry puts it, "[Y]ou maintain that the act of carrying out a crime is always accompanied by illness" (Dostoevsky 258). (Raskolnikov previews this argument early in the novel, wondering in the run-up to his murder of the old woman whether "crime somehow by its peculiar nature is always accompanied by something akin to disease" [71].)

In this chapter, I want to dwell on this statement in arguing that for Raskolnikov and Dostoevsky, crime *is* accompanied by a "disease" that looks awfully similar to moral injury. Indeed, I stand with Chizh in arguing that Dostoevsky is a canny observer of abnormal psychology and that *Crime and Punishment* offers an accurate prefiguration of Shay's, Litz's, and Nash's sketches of moral injury. But Dostoevsky's insights do not end there. Indeed, we see in *Crime and Punishment* not only a detailed portrait of a morally injured man but, in the figure of Sonya, a model for how one might treat such injury. Sonya is the character most responsible for Raskolnikov's promising if incomplete psychological rehabilitation, and I argue that her approach mirrors the therapeutic strategies for moral injury that Litz et al. champion in their book *Adaptive Disclosure.*

Crime and Punishment famously opens in the run-up to a murder. The protagonist, Raskolnikov, is an impoverished law student who has dropped out of school and is months behind on rent. Even in the novel's opening pages, he is considering killing an old woman—a money lender to whom he has pawned some of his last possessions. The murder happens near the end of the novel's first part when Raskolnikov brings an axe to the woman's flat and hacks her to death in a scene whose explicit violence shocked Dostoevsky's contemporaries. Hiding in the apartment after the murder, Raskolnikov is surprised by the woman's younger sister, whom he also kills before staging a miraculous escape. The remaining five parts of the novel document both the murder investigation and Raskolnikov's slow psychic breakdown. (To this main narrative are appended two family dramas: one focusing on the relatives of the drunk Marmeladov, who is run over by a carriage, and the other on Raskolnikov's sister Dunya and her multiple suitors.) As Dostoevsky indicates in the letter to Katkov mentioned above, there is essentially no physical evidence linking the criminal to the crime, and he likely would get away with the murders if not for his increasingly erratic behavior. Eventually, sensing incorrectly that investigators are closing in, and crumbling under the weight of his wrongdoing, Raskolnikov confesses and accepts a sentence of hard labor in Siberia. Marmeladov's daughter follows him there, and the two finally fall in love.

It is Raskolnikov's erratic behavior after the killing—and the psychic torment that drives it—that is of interest to us here. As mentioned above, Raskolnikov argues in his essay on crime that wrongdoing is often accompanied by sickness, a thesis his own experience bears out. Indeed, almost every other major character describes the young student as ill after the murder is committed. Both Raskolnikov's sister Dunya and their mother see him as suffering from a "great illness" (204). Porfiry repeatedly makes similar observations and at one point counsels Raskolnikov to "watch out for your illness" (347). The murderer himself is certainly cognizant of it, at one point chalking his suffering up to the fact that "I'm very sick. . . . I've tormented and tortured myself, without knowing myself what I'm doing" (110). The nature of that sickness is mysterious, and there are physical elements: delirium, fever, restlessness. However, it is the physician Zossimov who is most articulate in identifying its nonphysical character. Repeatedly, Zossimov advances the theory that Raskolnikov has gone mad, but his diagnoses are more persuasive when he is more temperate: "Also, from his observations, the patient's illness had, apart from the poor material circumstances of the recent months of his life, some moral causes as well" (207). This diagnosis of Raskolnikov's illness—as having "moral" causes—comports with Bakhtin's understanding of Dostoevsky as an author who frequently inflicts "moral torture" on his characters (54).[2]

A collection of symptoms suggests that moral injury provides a helpful model for thinking about Raskolnikov's "torture." Prime among them are the student's repeated, strenuous outbursts of anger. One might presume that a man in Raskolnikov's circumstances would occasionally lose his poise, but Dostoevsky makes it clear that his outbursts are both excessive and difficult for him to contain. Even when speaking with Razumikhin, a man whose unfailing kindness toward Raskolnikov he neither requests nor deserves, the latter "snapped rudely and angrily, suddenly changing his tone. Anger was boiling up in him and he could not suppress it" (253). Indeed, through large swaths of the novel, Raskolnikov swings wildly from torpor to fury. It is Zossimov again who first notes Raskolnikov's new tendency to fly "into a rage at the slightest word" (223)—as he does with almost every character in the novel, even those who are closest to him.

But perhaps most confounding is his inability to conceal his anger in the presence of Porfiry. From early on Raskolnikov suspects that Porfiry may be on to him, but he is repeatedly unable to control his temper with the persistent detective—a point that Dostoevsky makes over and over again throughout the men's extended conversations. Raskolnikov's ire is surprisingly most apparent in their second talk, one that could be the most banal. The young student has come to Porfiry asking that the inspector keep tabs on a number of the pawned items in the old woman's possession at the time of her death; these trinkets, Raskolnikov says, have sentimental value. Yet throughout what ought to be a mundane chat, he can barely keep his cool, and Dostoevsky describes his attitude in extreme language: "Raskolnikov could not help himself and angrily flashed a glance at him, his black eyes burning with wrath. . . . Anger was boiling up in him and he could not suppress it" (251, 253). Later on, in a subsequent (and indeed testier) exchange with Porfiry, Raskolnikov considers resorting to violence, so great is his fury: "At times he wanted to hurl himself at Porfiry and strangle him on the spot. He had been afraid of this anger from the moment he entered. He was aware that his lips were dry, his heart was pounding, there was foam caked to his lips" (341). Outside the moral injury paradigm, these extreme fits of pique can feel either idiosyncratic or melodramatic; inside it, they make much more sense. Further, Dostoevsky's indication that Raskolnikov is "afraid of" the anger is further indication that he understands it as being somehow out of his control.

These uncontrollable fits of rage have the effect of driving Raskolnikov's friends and family away, and their absence enhances the student's solitude. Accordingly, Dostoevsky frequently characterizes his protagonist both as seeking solitude and as physically repelled by the presence of others—this despite the fact that he is surrounded by a handful of characters who seek energetically to ensure his mental and physical well-being. That his mother, his sister, Zossimov, his friend Razumikhin, and Sonya are all so devoted to him serves only to emphasize the decisiveness of his drive toward isolation. Indeed, Dostoevsky himself indicates in his letter to Katkov that Raskolnikov's solitude is both the primary and the most painful result of the young man's crime. He writes, "[T]he feeling of being cut off and isolated from humanity that he had experienced from the moment he committed the crime had been torturing him" (222).[3]

Raskolnikov first begins to feel the working of this "torture" just shortly after the murder, and Dostoevsky describes it as a unique feeling: "A dark sensation of tormenting, infinite solitude and estrangement suddenly rose to consciousness in his soul. . . . What was taking place in him was totally unfamiliar, new, sudden, never before experienced" (103). And while Raskolnikov is sometimes able to shake that "sensation" and rejoin the company of his fellow humans, the feeling persists throughout the novel. Past the book's halfway point, Dostoevsky describes Raskolnikov's new and in some ways more total estrangement from others, as Raskolnikov comes to be "confined" in a "hopeless and heavy solitude" (439). This confinement is sudden and oppressive, but when he breaks out of it, he successfully connects that sense of isolation with his psychological struggles. Speaking with Sonya, he worries that she too will both become totally isolated *and* begin to suffer psychologically: "[I]f you remain *alone*," he pleads with her, "you'll lose your mind, like me" (329). Yet even if Raskolnikov understands the danger that loneliness poses to his mental state, he persists in avoiding others—even after his sentencing and through his time in Siberia. At the work camp, he still "shunned everyone . . . the convicts in the prison did not like him . . . he kept silent for whole days at a time" (542–43). That he does so even after he has confessed—and received his punishment—only bolsters the argument that his suffering is driven primarily by moral and psychological (rather than legal) concerns.

Unfortunately for Raskolnikov, his fellow prisoners interpret this shunning as a sign of haughtiness and accordingly threaten him with physical violence. That he does little to dispel their suspicions and actually seems to invite their assaults is evidence of his lacking self-care, which is associated with moral injury. But his uninterest in maintaining his physical and mental health first shows up much earlier in the novel. When Porfiry sees him a few days after the killing, he exclaims pointedly, "Lord! How is it you take no care of yourself at all?" (344) This lack of self-care manifests itself in a number of ways. Most important, Raskolnikov doesn't eat. He seems mostly to subsist on sips of cold cabbage soup and old tea furtively given to him by his housekeeper. (As Mochulsky notes, Dostoevsky takes this element from his own life, as he wrote early drafts of *Crime and Punishment* hungry, in a flat where he was so behind on his rent that his German landlady no longer provided him with food [270]). Further, when he does come into money that might allow him to feed and clothe himself, he repeatedly gives it all away. Most notably, a number of characters marvel at the fact that when his mother sends him a few dozen rubles to help him get by, Raskolnikov immediately gives them to the Marmeladovs to help them pay for a funeral (220).

One might be tempted to explain this expenditure in terms of his generous spirit; after all, we have other examples of Raskolnikov's altruism. However, it also seems driven, at least in part, by a sort of pointless prodigality, which we see earlier in the novel when he simply throws money into the river (115). Near the book's end, such habits have led him to a state of almost total destitution: "His clothes were terrible: everything was dirty, torn, tattered, after a whole night out in the rain. His face was almost disfigured by weariness, bad weather, physical exhaustion" (512). It's no surprise, then, that he is given to fainting spells, fatigue, and fever. This passage describes arguably Raskolnikov's worst night; destitute and alone, he wanders Petersburg in a Shakespearean gale, and he later admits that he nearly kills himself that evening: he "walked many times by the Neva; that I remember. I wanted to end it there, but . . . I couldn't make up my mind" (517). Raskolnikov does not commit suicide, as some others who suffer from moral injury do. But his survival is not a foregone conclusion. As Mochulsky notes, an early draft of the novel has Raskolnikov killing himself with "a bullet in the forehead" (283).

Of course, this is almost exactly the fate that awaits Svidrigailov. Spurned by Dunya—and in possession of her gun—he shoots himself in the head near the novel's end. And though one might assume he does so because he has just been finally spurned by Dunya, Svidrigailov too might be morally injured. Certainly he has crimes on his conscience: he emotionally and physically abuses a servant who eventually kills himself as a result; he molests a young girl who meets the same fate; and Dostoevsky implies that Svidrigailov poisons his wife. Given these ghastly deeds, his own suicide does not come as a surprise. Yet these facts are not irrelevant to an analysis of Raskolnikov's own pain. Indeed, as many have noted—Svidrigailov included—the two men are mirror images.[4] So Svidrigailov's journey is a sort of path-not-taken for Raskolnikov, a quite plausible alternate reality for the young student. I will return to this similarity below.

As is the case with other characters discussed in this book, Raskolnikov's inability to care for himself springs in part from his own demoralization, a damaging and durable negative evaluation of himself; indeed, Raskolnikov after the murder tends to think of himself, rather than his act, as reprehensible. A handful of passages suffice to demonstrate the trend. Unburdening himself to his sister, he mutters, "I'm a vile man, Dunya" (517). Then, just a few pages later and shortly before his confession, he thinks to himself, "I'm wicked, I see that. . . . [W]hy do they love me so, when I'm unworthy of it!" (520) He identifies the source of his "wickedness" when speaking to Sonya: "I have a wicked heart, Sonya; take note of that, it can explain a lot. That's why I came, because I'm wicked" (414). Note that here, as elsewhere in this book, the source of the wickedness is somehow biological; Raskolnikov's wicked heart both explains his behaviors and drives some of his acts.

One last, more pointed example most effectively demonstrates his demoralization. In one of the novel's most famous passages, Sonya urges Raskolnikov to a public display of repentance shortly after he reveals his crime to her: "Go now, this minute, stand in the crossroads, bow down, and first kiss the earth you've defiled, then bow to the whole world, on all four sides, and say aloud to everyone: '*I have killed!*'" (420; emphasis mine). Raskolnikov more or less dismisses her at the time but again considers her command when trying to get his courage up to formally confess. Yet tellingly, when he recites her words, he changes the final phrase: "Go to the crossroads, bow down to people, kiss the earth, because you have sinned before it as well, and say aloud to the whole world, 'I am a murderer'" (525). "I have killed" becomes "I am a murderer." Here again is that telling syntactical shift, this time drawn in stark relief by Raskolnikov's variation on Sonya's powerful theme. The killing has become part of his self-definition.

Yet as a close reading of the novel proves, the killing and its psychic effects also shape Raskolnikov's language and Dostoevsky's descriptions of the world in which he lives and moves. As with the other works examined in this book, the style of *Crime and Punishment* is shaped by the moral injury that its central murder produces, and as such, the novel's controlling mode is excess. Bakhtin says as much in *Problems of Dostoevsky's Poetics*, arguing that "[e]verything in this novel—the fates of people, their experiences and ideas—is pushed to its boundaries, everything is prepared, as it were, to pass over into its opposite . . . *is taken to the extreme, to its outermost limit*" (167; emphasis mine). And yet Dostoevsky indicates that the book's extremity is linked to its discussions of illness and disease. It is Svidrigailov who makes this connection most explicit when he characterizes "disease" as one of a family of things that "is bound to go beyond measure" (470). This is an apt description of the most famous "disease" in the novel, the "trichinae" that sweeps across the whole world in Raskolnikov's dream in the epilogue:

> In his illness he had dreamed that the whole world was doomed to fall victim to some terrible, as yet unknown and unseen pestilence spreading to Europe from the depths of Asia. Everyone was to perish, except for certain, very few, chosen ones. Some new trichinae had appeared, microscopic creatures that lodged themselves in men's bodies. But these creatures were spirits, endowed with reason and will. Those who received them into themselves immediately became possessed and mad. But never, never had people considered themselves so intelligent and unshakeable in the truth as did these infected ones. Never had they thought their judgments, their scientific conclusions, their moral convictions and beliefs more unshakeable. Entire settlements, entire cities and nations would be infected and go mad. Everyone became anxious, and no one understood anyone else; each thought the

truth was contained in himself alone, and suffered looking at others, beat his breast, wept, and wrung his hands. They did not know whom or how to judge, could not agree on what to regard as evil, what as good. They did not know whom to accuse, whom to vindicate. (547)

It would be going too far to say that this "trichinae" is moral injury, even if some of the pestilence's symptoms are quite familiar, notably isolation ("no one understood anyone else") and the "unshakeable" quality of victims' moral valuations. Yet what we do have in this passage are clear examples of the three major excess tropes associated with writing about moral injury and its antecedents. We have hyperbole: "*Everyone* was to perish"; "*never, never* had people considered themselves so intelligent." We have sublimity in the figure of a natural world that menaces with world-ending plagues hiding just beyond view. And we have signs of solitude: "each thought the truth was contained in himself alone." Indeed, this is a representative passage, as the three tropes often associated with moral injury show up repeatedly throughout the narrative.

It is once again Zossimov who notices Raskolnikov's use of hyperbole after the murders. Though he calls his patient's malady by a different name—monomania—he correctly identifies one of moral injury's main effects on the sufferer's thought and speech: "[T]hese monomaniacs turn a drop into an ocean" (212). And there are many moments in which Raskolnikov does just that, turning sprinkles into deluges. Dostoevsky gives us a representative example in the early part of chapter 2, as Raskolnikov begins to drive himself away from society. He initially does so because of an increasing disgust at the thought of other humans, a "boundless, almost physical loathing for everything he met or saw around him, an obstinate, spiteful, hate-filled loathing. *All* the people he met were repulsive to him—their faces, their walk, their movements were repulsive" (110; emphasis mine). Dostoevsky often puts such hyperbolic language in Raskolnikov's mouth when the young man is trying to express antisocial feelings. In similar fashion, he speaks of his animus toward Porfiry in the most extreme terms: "[H]e hated him beyond measure, infinitely" (332).

Here and elsewhere, Raskolnikov's misanthropy burns hot, but his estrangement from others is as often a source of cool sorrow or terror. At one point, sensing a break between himself and his mother after he lies to her, he fears that he will be totally cut off from her and everyone else: "[N]ot only would he never have the chance to talk all he wanted, but that it was no longer possible for him to *talk* at all, with anyone, about anything, ever" (229). Such exaggerated language about the length of his estrangement is echoed later in the book, when Raskolnikov imagines his pain stretching on forever: "Some particular anguish had begun telling in him lately. . . . [T]here came from it a breath of something permanent, eternal, a presentiment of unending years of this cold, deadening anguish, a presentiment of some eternity on 'a square foot of space'" (426).

The last piece of this quote—this "square foot of space"—refers back to one of Raskolnikov's reflections from earlier in the book:

"Where was it," Raskolnikov thought as he walked on, "where was it that I read about a man condemned to death saying or thinking, an hour before his death, that if he had to live somewhere high up on a cliffside, on a ledge so narrow that there was room only for his two feet—and with the abyss, the ocean, eternal darkness, eternal solitude, eternal storm all around him—and had to stay like that, on a square foot of space, an entire lifetime, a thousand years, an eternity—it would be better to live so than to die right now! Only to live, to live, to live! To live, no matter how—only to live!" (158)

At this point, not long after the murder, this "square foot" seems like an alluring provocation; even a life in such constrained cir-cumstances strikes Raskolnikov as preferable to death. Yet as the narrative unfolds, the image takes on a more menacing cast as Raskolnikov returns to it over and over again. And as it turns from a symbol of hope to one of despair, its sublimity becomes more apparent. Those familiar with Burke would see this as an exemplary description of the classic sublime, with its vertiginous heights, craggy rock face, inky night, and battering storm; the Turner painting produces itself. Of course, *Crime and Punishment* is a paradigmatic city novel, one that is to nineteenth-century Petersburg what *Ulysses* is to early twentieth-century Dublin. So visions of nature are fleeting. But when Dostoevsky does show us the natural world, it often looks mysterious, ominous, and threatening.

Take, for instance, one of the few times that Raskolnikov's wan-derings do send him outside the city limits. Even this brief brush with the countryside is unnerving—so much so that it sends him scurrying back to the city: "[I]t had happened that he would leave town, go out to the high road, once he even went as far as a lit-tle wood; but the more solitary the place was, the stronger was his awareness as of someone's near and disquieting presence, not frightening so much as somehow vexing, so that he would hur-riedly return to the city" (441). Instead of providing solace, this "little wood" feels haunted, distressing. We get a more explicit vi-sion of the sublime on the night of Svidrigailov's suicide while Raskolnikov wanders the city. That evening, Petersburg is racked by once-in-a-generation storms that threaten to flood the city. These storms pummel and drench Raskolnikov, but their effect on Svidrigailov is even more pronounced. "The water's rising," he thinks to himself. "Towards morning it will flood all the lower places, the streets; it will pour into the basements and cellars, the cellar rats will float up, and amid rain and wind people, cursed and drenched, will begin transferring their stuff to the upper floors" (507–8). Here, the rains are dangerous, and the figure of the rat corpses bubbling up from the basements renders the deluge both eerie and deadly.

Of course, the repeating image of the "square foot of space" is also an obvious sign of solitude, of which the novel features many others. Sometimes the solitude takes the form of a kind of isolating miasma, as in an extended version of a quotation previously mentioned: "[I]t was as if fog suddenly fell around him and confined him in a hopeless and heavy solitude" (439). Elsewhere, Dostoevsky uses surgical imagery to make a similar point about Raskolnikov's isolation: "It seemed to him that at that moment he had cut himself off, as with scissors, from everyone and everything" (115). And at other times, Dostoevsky puts Raskolnikov's loneliness in numerical terms. Speaking to his sister, Raskolnikov comments on the chasm that has opened up between them: "It's as if I were looking at you from a thousand miles away" (231). Dostoevsky uses such symbols to accentuate the "feeling of being cut off" that the author characterizes as defining Raskolnikov. But again, Dostoevsky's pronoun use serves a similar purpose, and the first person dominates as Raskolnikov wallows in his pain. Here is just one representative passage in the extended chapter during which the student confesses his crimes to Sonya:

> *I* endured all, all the torment of all this babble, Sonya, and *I* longed to shake it all off my back: *I* wanted to kill without casuistry, Sonya, to kill *for myself, for myself alone*! *I* didn't want to lie about it *even to myself*! It was not to help my mother that *I* killed—nonsense! *I* did not kill so that, having obtained means and power, *I* could become

a benefactor of mankind. Nonsense! *I* simply killed—killed *for my-self, for myself alone.* (419; emphasis mine)[5]

The first-person "I"s again pile up, but Raskolnikov's repetition of the crucial phrase—"for myself, for myself alone"—is so emphatic as to be almost inartful. Yet this fourfold iteration of the word "myself," punctuated twice by "alone," suggests once more that the murder has pushed him into solipsism.

The isolation of morally injured individuals represents a significant challenge for those who might try to help them. And in *Crime and Punishment*, a number of characters try valiantly to break through to Raskolnikov. Yet none is so persistent—or so effective—as Sonya. Indeed, I contend that she embodies some of the best practices currently available in the still-developing field of moral injury treatment. As suggested in chapter 1, there is still real debate about whether treatment strategies currently in use with trauma patients (notably cognitive processing therapy and prolonged exposure) can help those suffering from moral injury. I am not qualified to weigh in on this debate, but I can say that *Crime and Punishment* suggests that Dostoevsky was thinking about effective means of addressing the pain of perpetration more than a century ago. Or, to be more specific, I contend that in her dealings with Raskolnikov, Sonya models some of the treatment strategies laid out by Brett Litz and his team in *Adaptive Disclosure*—the first comprehensive effort to develop a unique treatment model for moral injury.[6] We reviewed Litz et al.'s model in chapter 1 but will expand on it in the following reading of Sonya's interactions with Raskolnikov.

Adaptive disclosure starts with the suggestion that morally injured individuals must work to avoid a variety of maladaptive coping strategies. We've already spent ample time focusing on the most common one: demoralization, or the tendency of morally injured individuals to see discrete bad acts as evidence that they are themselves bad. But Litz et al. discuss another: "excessive assimilation," in which morally injured individuals come to see their bad acts as somehow *acceptable* in a larger context (*Adaptive* 118). Take as an example the service member who roughs up an innocent family when mistakenly raiding the wrong house in a sweep for terrorists. The service member using this coping strategy might explain away such a bad act by letting it get lost in the perceived acceptability of a larger counterinsurgency campaign. Or as Litz et al. put it, "Service members or veterans who use this coping strategy may say to themselves, in effect, 'The military is good and just, and I am good and just, so what I did must also be good and just'" (118). Of course, this is a dastardly brand of utilitarianism that excuses just about any act by putting it in the context of some greater good. According to Litz et al., "This can be a slippery slope of negation of wrongdoing, leading to increasingly immoral behavior, if for no other reason than to find the limits of this newly expanded view of right and wrong" (118). One senses that in *Crime and Punishment* Raskolnikov is frequently falling into just such a maladaptive coping strategy. Remember that it is unclear even in the epilogue whether Raskolnikov has come to see his murders as "wrong." Throughout the book, he tries to justify them in terms of the worldview he promulgates in his article on crime. He does so at some great length in the midst of his confession to Sonya:

> The thing is that I once asked myself this question: how would it have been if Napoleon, for example, had happened to be in my place, and didn't have Toulon, or Egypt, or the crossing of Mont Blanc to start his career, but, instead of all these beautiful and monumental things, had quite simply some ridiculous old crone,

a leginstrar's widow, whom on top of that he had to kill in order to filch money from her trunk (for his career, you understand)—well, so, could he have made himself do it if there was no other way out? Wouldn't he have shrunk from it because it was so unmonumental and . . . and sinful? Well, I tell you, I suffered a terribly long time over this "question," so that I was terribly ashamed when I finally realized (somehow all at once) not only that he would not shrink, but that it wouldn't even occur to him that it was unmonumental . . . and he wouldn't understand at all what there was to shrink from. And if there was indeed no other path for him, he'd up and throttle her before she could make a peep, without a moment's thoughtfulness! . . . So I, too . . . came out of my thoughtfulness. . . . I throttled her . . . following the example of my authority. . . . And that's exactly how it was! (415)

Many critics and philosophers have written scores of pages debating whether or not Raskolnikov's ideas here have any merit, but the moral injury lens allows us to see them for what they really are: "excessive assimilation." He is trying to manage his moral injury by trying to convince himself that his crime was actually *right*. The logic of his thinking is quite beside the point, because it is less a cogent philosophy than a tattered bandage he is trying to press on a wound in his soul. Yet this strategy has some chilling ramifications, as it might end in the assumption that certain crimes are not only acceptable but laudable. Raskolnikov flirts with this end when he calls the old moneylender a "useless, nasty, pernicious louse" (416).

Litz et al. argue that in such situations, it is necessary for clinicians to affirm—firmly but tactfully—the badness of the bad act, and to keep the morally injured individual from assimilating or rationalizing the ethical breach. As they write, "It is important to remember that holding on to the idea of a moral self or a moral code may require that a bad act be judged as such" (*Adaptive* 118).

In other words, moral repair demands the maintenance of an intact moral system. Sonya is firm in doing so for Raskolnikov, and whenever he starts spinning off into rationalization, she pulls him back by insistently reminding him of the true nature of his crime. At one point, as Raskolnikov begins to attest to a right to disregard certain moral rules, Sonya stops him:

> "Am I a trembling creature, or do I have the *right* . . ."
> "To kill? The right to kill?"
> [. . .]
> "I went only *to try*. . . . You should know that!"
> "And you killed! Killed!" (419)

Note first Sonya's diction: situating the murder at a particular moment in time, she says, "[Y]ou killed"—not, as Raskolnikov might, "You are a killer." Nonetheless, Sonya does not let Raskolnikov move the fact of the murder into the context of an abstract discussion of rights; if he is to regain his moral balance, he must come to relearn the badness of his crime, and here Sonya affirms it. Elsewhere, when Raskolnikov once again asserts that the moneylender is a "louse," Sonya corrects him:

> "I only killed a louse, Sonya, a useless, nasty, pernicious louse."
> "A human being—a louse!"
> "Not a louse, I know it myself." (416)

This last line suggests that Sonya's approach is working at some level to remind Raskolnikov of moral truths that he already knows.

And yet clinicians seeking to remind morally injured individuals of the evil of their acts walk a fine line, because if they push too hard, their clients may fall again into demoralization. Litz et al. argue that clinicians must have a light touch, proposing salutary readings of relevant acts without pressing too hard: "The goal is to 'plant seeds,' encourage the consideration of other possible interpretations, and kick-start a process of accommodating transgression without overaccommodating evil and negating any possibility of a positive and good self" (*Adaptive* 119). Sonya is particularly effective at "planting seeds" without coming on too strong. In the confession scene and after, she tends to let Raskolnikov talk, gently nudging him toward healthier interpretations of his plight with brief phrases and single words. Indeed, after she follows him to Siberia for his hard-labor sentence, she is unwilling to pressure him with either her words or her presence. Though she occasionally visits him at the camp, at other times she simply comes to the gates so that he can see her and feel her presence: "She had often come to the hospital courtyard, under the windows, especially towards evening, or sometimes just to stand in the yard for a short while and look at least from afar at the windows of the ward" (548). Indeed, even Raskolnikov is impressed at her light touch. At one point in the epilogue, he admits that he expected her to "hound" him and "forc[e] books on him" (550); she doesn't, and her tact lets him approach her when he is ready.

However, tact doesn't equal distance, and Litz et al. argue that it is crucial for the therapist "to be fully emotionally present" so that the client may approach "horrifying thoughts and feelings in the presence of an accepting other" (*Adaptive* 121). Doing so is difficult when the moral breach in question is particularly disturbing, and the therapist must avoid disgust and condemnation. Sonya is quite effective in this respect, and she practices both presence and acceptance even as she becomes aware of the violence of Raskolnikov's deed. As the revelation hits, she reacts by moving closer to the murderer, both comforting and embracing him. Dostoevsky makes sure to point out the physical proximity of Sonya as Raskolnikov begins his confession; at the beginning, Sonya "quickly moved closer to him, seized both his hands, and, squeezing them tightly with her thin fingers, as in a vise, again began looking fixedly in his face" (411). Neither her body nor her gaze drifts, and even as she comes to understand that the student is also a killer, her impulse is to maintain contact; she "sat down again beside him, almost touching him, shoulder to shoulder" (411). Her willingness to accompany Raskolnikov to Siberia is the most dramatic sign of her co-presence, and it serves as a source of strength for Raskolnikov both as he turns himself in and as he accepts his sentence: she "had accompanied him throughout his sorrowful procession. Raskolnikov felt and understood in that moment, once and for all, that Sonya was now with him forever" (526). Sonya goes well beyond the therapist's responsibility in her willingness to take on his exile, but her decision to do so is a sign of an acceptance that, for Litz et al., serves as a crucial foundation for "the possibility of growth and continued movement" (*Adaptive* 121).

One of the reasons that acceptance and presence are so important is that they remind morally injured individuals that while they have done wrong, they are also both lovable and capable of good. Adaptive disclosure has as one of its most important aims the championing of the difficult truth that "worthwhile people do terrible things" (Litz et al., *Adaptive* 121). It advances a complex view of the human personality as a storehouse for both good and bad acts. For many, this is a tough pill to swallow, but such a revelation can help morally injured individuals put their moral breaches in the context of long lives that also feature admirable acts and character traits. As Litz et al. write, "The fact that someone did something bad does not render any other good he or she has done in his or her life null and void, nor does it change who he or she is at the core or who he or she might become over the course of life" (124). Interestingly, it is Svidrigailov who makes this point with the most clarity in *Crime and Punishment*. Talking with Dunya shortly before his suicide, he reminds her that Raskolnikov's crime needn't shape the entirety of his life: "And as for the murder, he'll still have time to do many good deeds, so it will all be made up for; calm yourself. He still may be a great man" (492). Indeed, in the epilogue, the narrator brings to light the fact that Raskolnikov is already responsible for "many good deeds"—some of them quite dramatic. During his school years, he provided financial support for a sick fellow student who couldn't afford his tuition and board. Even more admirably, he cared for the student's ailing father after the young man's death and even provided for the old man's burial after he too died. These deeds come out during Raskolnikov's trial, along with the fact that he once saved two children from a burning building (537). That Dostoevsky reveals them only in the "healing" part of the novel—after the murder, after the trial, and once Raskolnikov's sentence has begun—suggests that they might have a salutary effect on him as he starts to rebuild his life. Indeed, they underline the truth that even this convicted double murderer is a complex moral being capable of both heinous evil and remarkable good.

Of course, healing from moral injury may well require not only acknowledging previous goods but creating new ones, and Litz et al. note that for some clients, making a plan for future atoning acts can provide hope and strength (*Adaptive* 125). The goal is not to erase the bad deed—such an erasure would be both impossible and damaging—but rather to reaffirm the morally injured individuals' potential for good. It is telling, then, that the closing lines of *Crime and Punishment* gesture toward just such a future good for Raskolnikov: in the book's penultimate paragraph, the narrator says that the student "did not even know that a new life would not be given to him for nothing, that it still had to be dearly bought to be paid for with a great future deed" (551). But the suggestion here is simple: continued benevolence can help with the gradual renewal of the morally injured, even those whose suffering results from the bloodiest of deeds. Further, in this quotation, Dostoevsky also indicates that the double murderer Raskolnikov is also quite capable of a "great future deed." In other words, *Crime and Punishment* promulgates a salutary anthropology in which one bad act does not destine one to be forever a villain. Rather, for Dostoevsky, as for Litz, people are morally complex and eminently capable of both charity and crime—often in the same lifetime. To heal, Raskolnikov must accept this difficult fact.

But my sense is that Dostoevsky, in drawing his protagonist in such vexing psychic detail, is challenging his reader to do the same: to accept a character who can both slaughter defenseless old women *and* selflessly care for the dying father of a schoolmate. In this respect, *Crime and Punishment* is not only a book about caring for those suffering the pain of perpetration; it is also a book that might be therapeutic for the morally injured. For in asking readers to live with and believe in such a morally complicated protagonist, Dostoevsky also asks us to subscribe to a worldview that would make one more resilient to moral injury. To wit, the belief that "worthwhile" people can do bad things is a hedge against MI, and it is a hedge that Dostoevsky erects in painstaking detail with the character of Raskolnikov.

Notes

1. So great is Bakhtin's influence that it inspires an entire monograph on the theorist's effect on Dostoevsky studies: Malcolm V. Jones's *Dostoyevsky after Bakhtin: Readings in Dostoyevsky's Fantastic Realism.*

2. Chizh comes closest to my own reading of the novel in arguing that some characters—though not Raskolnikov himself—suffer from "moral insanity."

He borrows the term from the nineteenth-century British psychologist James Pritchard and says it applies best to Svidrigailov (Rice 208).

3. Among others, Mochulsky (303), Allan (142), and Tucker (221) all point out the importance of this theme.

4. Breger calls Svidrigailov Raskolnikov's "double" (42)—Bakhtin his "parodic double" (89).

5. We see a similar passage in one of Raskolnikov's early conversations with Dunya: "I wanted to tell you . . . as I was coming here . . . I wanted to tell you, mama . . . and you, Dunya, that it's better if we part ways for a while. I'm not feeling well, I'm not at ease. . . . I'll come myself afterwards . . . when I can. I think of you and love you. . . . Leave me! Leave me alone! I decided on it even before. . . . I decided on it for certain. . . . Whatever happens to me, whether I perish or not, I want to be alone. Forget me altogether" (313).

6. Curiously, the novel seems to discard a treatment approach akin to cognitive processing therapy (CPT)—as do Litz et al. in their discussions of moral injury treatment. Recall for a moment that practitioners of CPT (and its cousin, cognitive behavioral therapy [CBT]) take as a starting point the notion that the pain of trauma springs from incorrect thinking about the traumatic event (or MIE). They further suggest that careful, rational reevaluation of these false beliefs can help ease psychic pain. As mentioned previously, Litz et al. are suspicious of such an approach to moral injury, as they believe that the pain associated with it may not be altogether irrational; they write, "As a point of departure from conventional CBT approaches, adaptive disclosure does not assume that anguish, shame, and distress are necessarily caused by distorted thinking" (*Adaptive* 119). *Crime and Punishment* seems to evince a similar suspicion. As one character puts it, "[D]o you know that in Paris serious experiments have already been performed with regard to the possibility of curing mad people by working through logical conviction alone? . . . [T]he basic idea is that there's no specific disorder in a mad person's organism, but that madness is, so to speak, a logical error, an error of judgment, a mistaken view of things" (424). The speaker trails off, and Raskolnikov mutters, "Life would be too easy that way" (424).

4

"The Vices of Our Whole Generation"

COLLECTIVE MORAL INJURY IN *THE FALL*

In a 1944 editorial written for the French Resistance journal *Combat*, Albert Camus weighed in on the case of Louis Renault, the head of the massive automobile manufacturer that shared his last name. That year, Renault was apprehended by post-Vichy French authorities and stood accused of collaborating with German occupiers. The charges were simple: Renault kept his factories open during the war and allegedly provided billions of francs' worth of supplies for the Wehrmacht (Camus, *Combat* 47). Like many other accused collaborators, Renault defended himself by saying that he cooperated with the German forces in order to survive; anyone else would have done the same. In his editorial, Camus disagreed, arguing among other things that Renault was ethically—and perhaps even legally—bound to do more, to resist more energetically. Here is the piece's conclusion:

> To speak in such terms is new and lends itself to ridicule. There would be less laughter if these ideas became law and if proportional responsibilities found some juridical translation. During those four dreadful years all Frenchmen were witnesses to a crime not foreseen by any law (and in saying this we are weighing our words carefully): *the crime of not doing enough.* French big business is guilty in our eyes because it *refused to risk anything.* (48; emphasis mine)

There's no missing the starkness of Camus's suggestion: witnessing evil and doing little to resist is not only objectionable; it is potentially criminal. He even imagines a law that one might implement in order to prosecute those guilty of this "new" crime.

The notion that there is something ethically wrong with "refusing to risk" is one that Camus returned to occasionally throughout his work for *Combat*. Later, as he reflected on the atrocities of World War II, it became apparent to him that acknowledging or condemning evil is not sufficient; one must do more. As he wrote in his 1946 series "Neither Victims nor Executioners," "[W]hile there are many people nowadays who condemn violence in their heart of hearts, there aren't many willing to recognize that this obliges them to reconsider the way they think and act" (272). Indeed, there is some evidence that Camus himself had regrets about "not doing enough" during the war. Though the author is frequently praised for his writing for *Combat*—by many counts the preeminent organ of the Resistance press—he would sometimes acknowledge that his work for the Resistance was negligible when compared to that of others; at one point, he admitted that his "'little activity' in the Resistance seemed to him 'derisory next to that of some of my comrades who were real combatants'" (Todd 171). There is even some evidence that he came to see the "littleness" of his activity as something more (or less) than "derisory." As the forties wore on, Camus became more and more disillusioned with Marxist-inspired Communism as an answer to the world's problems. While he certainly sympathized with the working class, he came to believe that Marxism was a hyperutilitarian political system that would gladly sacrifice lives in pursuit of the classless utopia. Hence, in the years following the war, when a friend became a Marxist, Camus said to him, "'So you will be a murderer.' The friend replied, 'I've already been one.' Camus said, 'Me too,

but I don't want to be one anymore'" (237). Camus's reply is gnomic, but one interpretation of his self-accusation suggests that
he saw his "derisory" work for the Resistance as both deadly and
ultimately similar to the criminal inaction of the collaborationist
carmaker Renault.

Whether or not such speculation holds up, we may say with
confidence that the crime of not doing enough is one that continued to animate Camus's thinking and writing throughout
the rest of his relatively brief career as an author. In this chapter,
I contend that the criminal nature of refusing to risk is the central
concept driving Camus's late novel *The Fall*. Indeed, in the decisive
moment of that book, its main character, Clamence, commits the
crime of doing too little. Further, Clamence suffers for his failure
and, I would argue, is morally injured by it. Yet we may go one
step further, for there is ample evidence in *The Fall* to support the
claim that from Clamence's point of view, an entire generation
of Europeans is both similarly culpable and similarly injured by
their unwillingness to risk anything for those who suffered most
in those bloody middle years of the twentieth century. Hence,
I also want to suggest that Camus's novel sets forth a preliminary
theory of collective moral injury, in which an entire community—
considered as a group—suffers in the wake of a massive ethical
lapse. In doing so, I build on the sociologist Kai Erikson's pioneering work on collective trauma.

The ethical reflections in Albert Camus's 1957 novel *The Fall* are
set off by a literal fall. Late one night, while wandering the streets
of Paris, Jean-Baptiste Clamence passes a woman standing alone
on a bridge crossing the Seine. As he moves off the bridge, he hears
a sequence of cries that follow a splash—presumably from the
woman throwing herself into the water below. Barely hesitating,

Clamence does nothing and pushes on, returning home and ignoring the papers the next morning. The rest of the novel is best understood as the character's reflections on the changes that fateful night wreaks on his psyche and worldview.

Shoshana Felman advances what has become a definitive reading of *The Fall* in *Testimony: Crises of Witnessing in Literature, Psychoanalysis, and History*, a pillar of literary trauma theory. For Felman, *The Fall* must be read as a follow-up to Camus's previous novel, *The Plague*. According to Felman, *The Plague* is primarily concerned with the possibility that one might accurately witness trauma—in this case, an actual plague that rips through a North African city. By contrast, *The Fall* is about a failure to witness trauma—namely, Clamence's failure to witness the anonymous woman's death. Felman describes Clamence's unwillingness to acknowledge or report her death in terms of a forcible silence: "Silence here is not a simple absence of an act of speech, but a positive avoidance—and erasure—of one's hearing, the positive *assertion* of a deafness, in the refusal not merely to answer but to *acknowledge*—and henceforth respond or *answer to*—what is being heard or witnessed" (Felman and Laub 183). Yet for Felman, Clamence's silence is also metonymically linked to Europeans' failure to effectively witness to the death of millions of Jews in the Holocaust: "*The Fall*, indeed, enacts the Holocaust as a radical *failure of representation*, in both senses of the word: failure of representation in the sense of *making present* the event; failure of representation in the sense of truly *speaking for* the victim, whose voicelessness no voice can represent" (197). In its focus on silence rather than language, on "voicelessness" and unspeakability, Felman's reading is very much in keeping with other early trauma-theoretical readings of literature, among them the studies by Caruth and Geoffrey Hartman mentioned previously.[1] Indeed, in a reading of Felman's essay, Colin Davis affirms that *The Fall* is "undoubtedly about trauma" and that "it is not difficult . . . to make the case for the relevance of *La Chute* to trauma studies" (39).

And yet, as Daniel Just argues, "Clamence does not seem as traumatized as Felman asserts" (900). Likewise, LaCapra would rather see Clamence not as a victim but as an "implicated bystander" (*History* 76).[2] But perhaps even this claim is not pointed enough, for Clamence *chooses* to stand by while the woman dies; to wit, he is less "implicated" than at least partially culpable in her passing. Indeed, a close analysis of Clamence's long narrative reveals that he is psychologically scarred by what he comes to see as a discrete ethical lapse—by his willing failure to stop a tragic event. Or, in the terms Camus uses in *Combat*, Clamence is guilty of not doing enough. As such, the character comes to understand his inaction on the bridge as a moral error that haunts him even as he tries to flee it:

> I realized, calmly as you resign yourself to an idea the truth of which you have long known, that the cry which had sounded over the Seine behind me years before had never ceased, carried by the river to the waters of the Channel, to travel throughout the world, across the limitless expanse of the ocean, and that it had waited for me there until the day I had encountered it. (108)

The cry follows and torments him because it is the aural symbol of his crime, and its effects are recognizable as the full array of moral injury symptoms.

Clamence's moral injury drives behavioral changes that conform with the concept as explained in previous chapters. First, his conduct exemplifies two of the ailment's main symptoms: anger and poor self-care. We see evidence of the first in an unexpected altercation with a fellow motorist. Stuck behind a frustrated man on a stalled motorcycle, an increasingly angry Clamence leaves his own car to attack the biker: "[F]illed with a healthy rage . . . I got out of my car with the intention of thrashing this coarse individual" (52). However, when another motorist comes to the motorcyclist's aid, Clamence turns his anger on this new "d'Artagnan" with the intention of "giving a drubbing to the idiot who had addressed me" (53). Both men leave when the traffic snarl eases, but we see evidence here that Clamence's impulse in trying to resolve relatively mundane conflicts is physical violence.

This willingness to resort to brawling is also evidence of his increasingly poor self-care. Indeed, in the years following the night on the Seine, Clamence slips into a life of alcoholism and promiscuity, pushing his body to the limit both physically and sexually. He drinks gin like water, referring to the spirit as "the sole glimmer of light in this darkness" (12). When he is not thoroughly drunk, he frequents brothels: "Despairing of love and of chastity, I at last bethought myself of debauchery. . . . [L]ying late at night between two prostitutes and drained of all desire, hope ceases to be a torture, you see. . . . I went to bed with harlots and drank for nights on end" (102). Later on, he describes the thin consolation these pursuits allow: "Alcohol and women provided me, I admit, the only solace of which I was worthy. . . . [T]rue debauchery is liberating because it creates no obligations. In it you possess only yourself" (103). But the solace is limited, and he soon begins contemplating suicide—another key symptom of moral injury. Earlier in the novel, he laments, "Don't think for a minute that your friends will telephone you every evening, as they ought to, in order to find out if this doesn't happen to be the evening when you are deciding to commit suicide" (31). Later, he even fantasizes about killing himself to avenge himself on those friends, "to play a trick on them, to punish them, in a way" (74). However, he quickly realizes that at this point in his life, he has no one to punish: "I realized I had no friends" (74). Indeed, his friendlessness exemplifies another of the moral injury symptoms he exhibits: social withdrawal.

By his own admission, Clamence before the fall is a gregarious, affable, social being. He not only enjoys the company of others but is eloquent and socially adept. However, after that fateful night on the Seine, he begins to remove himself from the company of others. He first abandons his Paris set, settling instead in Amsterdam and spending most of his time drinking at a woebegone bar at the edge of the city. Further, even from this lonely outpost, he seeks more emphatic solitude, taking a boat out on the foggy waters surrounding the city, where all land is invisible. His goal, it seems, is near-total isolation: "No human beings, above all, no human beings. You and I alone facing the planet at last deserted" (72–73). Moreover, the narrative itself enacts Clamence's withdrawal: the book includes only his words. There is no narrator and no dialogue by other characters—even though Clamence's long monologue assumes the presence of an unnamed auditor. In brief, Clamence is talking to someone, but Camus never gives us any of the other person's words—nor even, really, absolute confirmation that he exists. (An extreme reading of *The Fall* has an addled Clamence speaking for 150 pages into the void.) In sum, Clamence is, narratively speaking, utterly alone.

Yet the night on the bridge affects not only Clamence's behaviors but also his attitudes. Before witnessing the young woman's suicide, Clamence has a strong sense of himself as an ethical being living in a world with a sound, predictable moral structure. He is well-mannered and courteous. He takes pride in his altruistic impulses, helping the infirm cross streets and giving generously to charity. He speaks convincingly of the support he draws from the sound ethical structure of his universe: "The feeling of the law, the satisfaction of being right, the joy of self-esteem, *cher monsieur*, are powerful incentives for keeping us upright or keeping us moving forward" (18). And in truth, these forces not only keep Clamence moving forward; they give him great pleasure: "I enjoyed that part of my nature which reacted so appropriately to the widow and the orphan" (20). Yet after his moral injury, Clamence's views of himself and the world change significantly. First, he comes to see his charity and goodwill as both self-serving and superficial, and he grows ashamed of the pride he takes in his good works. Furthermore, he eventually characterizes his altruism as a thin veil masking a will to power: "I was eager to get my revenge, to strike and conquer. As if my true desire were not to be the most intelligent or most generous creature on earth, but only to beat anyone I wanted, to be the stronger, in short, and in the most elementary way . . . I discovered in myself sweet dreams of oppression" (55).

As he ruminates on these themes, he comes to see the entire world as suffering from a similar malady: each and every one of us is immoral—is guilty—but all of us are buoyed by delusions of impunity. For Clamence, this false feeling of innocence is common if not universal: "The idea that comes most natural to man, as if from his very nature, is the idea of his innocence" (81). And yet he comes to believe that the exact opposite is true. The central tenet of his new "faith" is a belief in universal guilt: "[W]e cannot assert the innocence of anyone, whereas we can state with certainty the guilt of all. Every man testifies to the crime of all the others" (110). Indeed, so swayed is he by this revelation that he alters the nature of his legal vocation. Where before Clamence defended "widows and orphans," he now takes on the cases of real criminals: pimps, thieves, and murderers. He explains, "If pimps and thieves were invariably sentenced, all decent people would get to thinking they themselves were constantly innocent, *cher monsieur*. And in my opinion . . . that's what must be avoided above all" (41). Clamence begins by seeing his act as bad but ends up thinking of *himself* as bad—and then spreads that self-condemnation over the entire world.

Clamence's moral injury also affects the way he assigns blame. As mentioned previously, Litz et al. note that morally injured individuals are more likely to heal if they can explain the event to themselves as specific, external, and "not stable" ("Moral" 701). In other words, afflicted perpetrators can recover if they can come to see their bad actions as related to a physical, temporal, and situational context, rather than to some enduring character flaw. Unfortunately for Clamence, he is initially dubious of context-specific explanations and speaks of them dismissively: "[I]f you tell a criminal that his crime is not due to his nature or his character but to unfortunate circumstances, he will be extravagantly grateful to you" (81). Eventually he comes to reject such descriptions as mere excuses: "No excuses ever, for anyone; that's my principle at the outset. I deny the good intention, the respectable mistake, the indiscretion, the extenuating circumstance. With me there is no giving of absolution or blessing" (131). And as becomes apparent, there is neither absolution nor blessing for himself. He is unable to see his ethical lapses as related to anything other than humans' bone-deep, universal guilt, and thus he can find no forgiveness—either for himself or for anyone else.

Of course, this is language with which we have become familiar; Clamence sees his sin metastasizing so quickly as to be total, ubiquitous. As he tries to describe his sorrowful state, he struggles to keep up with the creeping growth of his sense of guilt, throwing paragraphs of uninterrupted speech at it. Hence, we have in *The Fall* a paradigmatic example of the moral injury monologue—of the never-sufficient effort to "say everything" about the self-inflicted wound and its effects. Accordingly, Clamence repeatedly admits to "letting [himself] go" with his speech (14). In language that recalls that of Coleridge's ancient mariner, he even lets on that his torrent of words extends beyond the book's covers. The five-day speech he delivers is just one iteration of a talk he has given dozens (or hundreds?) of times before—and that he will give again and again. But yet again, moral injury affects not only the quantity but the quality of a perpetrator's speech. Clamence admits as much himself, claiming that in the years following the fall, he begins to do some creative writing in which he adopts "the lyricism of the prison cell" (124). Such "lyricism" is a sort of poetics of guilt, and as in *Crime and Punishment*, this poetics encompasses the three tropes often associated with discussions of moral injury.

We first see these stylistic effects in Clamence's frequent use of hyperbole. It follows that Clamence's diction is full of superlatives and absolutes. When he finally faces his inadequacies, the revelation hits him with unbelievable force: "I received *all the wounds* at the same time and lost my strength *all at once. The whole universe* then began to laugh at me" (80; emphasis mine). Articulating his sins in a revealing "confession" to junior colleagues, he characterizes himself as peerless in his depravity: "I am free, shielded from your severities, yet who am I? A Louis XIV in pride, a billy goat for lust, a Pharaoh for wrath, a king of laziness" (95). If he was previously matchless in his charity, now he is matchless in his sin. And his final self-indictment is pithy and exaggerated: "I was the lowest of the low" (140). As this self-described worst of sinners turns his attention to the rest of the world, he observes wickedness everywhere and eternally. Eventually he comes to see *everyone* else as somehow complicit in his crimes: "I have no more friends; I have nothing but accomplices. To make up for this, their number has increased; they are the whole human race" (73). However, the "whole human race" is not merely an accessory to his sins; they are all guilty. As he states in the passage quoted earlier, "[W]e can state with certainty the guilt of all" (110).

This is the philosophical center of the novel, but it is also convincing evidence that Clamence suffers from a diagnosable psychic wound. Having hit rock bottom, Clamence reflects back on his happy, prelapsarian state. Yet even then, he continues to use hyperbolic language; before the fall, he says, "I recognized no equals. I always considered myself more intelligent than everyone else, as I've told you, but also more sensitive and more skillful, a crack shot, an incomparable driver, a better lover" (48). Later, describing his professional probity, he brags, "I *never* accepted a bribe, it goes without saying, and I *never* stooped either to any shady proceedings. . . . I *never* deigned to flatter any journalist. . . . I *never* charged the poor a fee and never boasted of it" (19–20; emphasis mine). In sum, if in the novel's present, Clamence is "lowest of the low," previously he was highest of the high. Among its other effects, MI drives one to adopt a harmfully simplistic worldview—suddenly one can only see charcoal black and lily white. As William Nash notes, those suffering "moral injury either conclude that 'none of this is my fault,' or 'it's all my fault'" (Wood, "Good"). Clamence's use of hyperbolic language suggests that he has fallen into such a linguistic and ethical trap.

His imagery is similarly excessive. Recognizing a threat from evil in his soul, he comes to see the world itself as threatening. Thus, he often borrows sublime images that fill a dangerous cosmos. For instance, human society is a school of piranhas: "You have heard, of course, of those tiny fish in the rivers of Brazil that attack the unwary swimmer by thousands and with swift little nibbles clean him up in a few minutes, leaving only an immaculate skeleton? Well, that's what their organization is" (7). However, Clamence now lives in a world where not only do flesh-eating fish champ at his heels, but even creatures once presumed docile take on an ominous cast. In an image that anticipates Hitchcock, the doves of Amsterdam blot out the skies above, bullying Clamence rather than comforting him: "See the huge flakes drifting against the windowpanes. It must be the doves, surely. They finally make up their minds to come down, the little dears; they are covering the waters and the roofs with a thick layer of feathers; they are fluttering at every window. What an invasion!" (145)

But it is not only the fauna of Clamence's world that frighten; the landscape itself is totally blighted. His description of the washed-out waterways surrounding Amsterdam becomes a fitting metaphor for his desolate, precarious position: "Everything horizontal, no relief; space is colorless, and life dead. Is it not universal obliteration, everlasting nothingness made visible? No human beings, above all, no human beings" (72). Indeed, for Clamence, Amsterdam is not only "universal obliteration" but hell itself. He later describes it as both the "extremity of this Europe" (144) and the last circle of Dante's inferno: "Have you noticed that Amsterdam's concentric canals resemble the circles of hell? . . . When one comes from the outside, as one gradually goes through those circles, life—and hence its crimes—becomes denser, darker. Here, we are in the last circle" (14). MI afflicts those who suffer it with a vision of the world as decaying and terrifying, and Clamence's imagery is further evidence that he now lives in this world.

Too often, however, Clamence feels isolated within that world, and that feeling shapes his language. Thus, we see much free (and knowing) play with first-person pronouns and numerous signs of solitude. To the first, Clamence is very aware of his heavy use of the word "I"—*je* in the French original. At first, he announces it as a sort of boast: "I, I, I is the refrain of my whole life, which could be heard in everything I said" (48). But this "refrain" soon turns from chant to dirge, and "I" becomes less a celebratory vaunt than a habit he can't break if he tries. Says Clamence just a few pages later, "I lived consequently without any other continuity than that, from day to day, of I, I, I" (50). The text of *The Fall* supports this observation. In a relatively brief book (roughly 30,000 words in the French original), Clamence uses some form of the French *je* no fewer than 1,100 times. Further, Clamence is quite attuned to his own linguistic style, and he claims to have precise control over his word choice. He characterizes his deployment of pronouns as a rhetorical strategy designed to implicate his audience: he articulates his "shames without losing sight of the effect I am producing, and saying: 'I was the lowest of the low.' Then imperceptibly I pass from the 'I' to the 'we.' When I get to 'This is what we are,' the trick has been played and I can tell them off. I am like them, to be sure; we are in the soup together" (140). To a certain extent, his claim is true. If we take the woman's fall as the rough geographical center of the novel (it happens on page 70 of the 147-page English translation by Justin O'Brien), we observe an appreciable increase in the number of second-person plural pronouns (the French *nous*) in the latter half.[3] Yet though Clamence promises that this rise will coincide with a fall in his use of the first-person pronoun, this prediction does not bear out. Indeed, we see forms of the pronoun *je* appear as frequently (if not more so) after the fall.[4] In sum, as Clamence "passes" to the second-person *nous*, the first-person *je* never passes away.

We see further evidence that Clamence is effectively trapped with himself in the novel's imagery, which echoes his solitude. *The Fall* is predominantly a city novel, and Camus often provides us with scenes of his protagonist wandering the streets of Paris or Amsterdam. However, Clamence notes that the life of the *flaneur* is a lonely one: "They wander, pretending to hasten toward the tired wife, the forbidding home. . . . Ah, *mon ami*, do you know what the *solitary creature* is like as he wanders in big cities?" (118; emphasis mine) Not unexpectedly, then, Clamence is effectively alone at the novel's crucial moments: when he hears the laugh on the bridge, "there were but few people on the quays" (38), and when he passes the woman who falls, he is the solitary witness (69). Later, when he rides on a boat and catches a glimpse of what he thinks is a drowning victim off in the distance, the scene is one of terrifying distance and isolation: "Suddenly, far off at sea, I perceived *a black speck on the steel-gray ocean*. I turned away at once and my heart began to beat wildly. When I forced myself to look, the black speck had disappeared" (108; emphasis mine).

Yet even when Clamence is not discussing the novel's main turning points—the moments that either cause or exacerbate his moral injury—his language is filled with symbols of loneliness and solitude. For instance, he claims to prefer islands to shores, isolated dots of land to sprawling continents: "What I like most in the world is Sicily . . . Java, too. . . . In a general way, I like all islands" (43). Later, when he speaks of a lie that is never corrected, he uses a metaphor that recalls the (illusory) drowning victim mentioned above: "[W]hat pretension to want to drag out into the full light of truth a paltry fraud, *lost in the sea of ages like a grain of sand on the ocean*?" (90; emphasis mine) But the most telling sign of solitude in Clamence's monologue comes in his metaphor for modern life: the little-ease. Here is his extended description:

> To be sure, you are not familiar with that dungeon cell that was called the little-ease in the Middle Ages. In general, one was forgotten there for life. That cell was distinguished from others by ingenious dimensions. It was not high enough to stand up in nor yet

wide enough to lie down in. . . . Every day through the unchang-
ing restriction that stiffened his body, the condemned man learned
that he was guilty. (109)

The little-ease is the novel's most memorable—and most thoroughly developed—metaphor, and it is also a powerful symbol of
solitary confinement on the tiniest possible scale.

All of these signs of solitude both confirm and enhance
Clamence's sense—and ours—of his increasing distance from society. However, he also believes that his situation is not unique.
Indeed, he argues that in some ways, all Europeans who survive
the war years are similarly tormented. Near the end of the book, he
notes that "*we* are lodged in the little-ease" (114; emphasis mine).
Or, as I will claim below, in *The Fall*, Clamence and all his com-
patriots suffer from what I want to call collective moral injury—a
kind of shared pain that results from failing to save the century's
many victims.

In his famous study of the psychological effects of the 1972 flood
at Buffalo Creek, West Virginia, the sociologist Kai Erikson pro-
poses the term "collective trauma" to describe the damage that
larger-scale disasters can do to social groups ("Trauma" 153–61).
In the simplest terms, Erikson argues that catastrophes may both
scar individual psyches and do lasting damage to the ties that bind,
weakening—if not totally dissolving—the links that hold society
together.[5] Collective trauma, he writes elsewhere, is "a blow to
the basic tissues of social life that damages the bonds attaching
people together and impairs the prevailing sense of communal-
ity" ("Notes" 460).[6] In the years since, psychologists and sociolo-
gists have verified the use value of Erikson's term. In a 2000 essay,
Suárez-Orozco and Robben argue that "large-scale violence and
massive trauma disintegrate trust in the social structures that

make human life possible" (5). And in a 2013 volume, Jack Saul notes that acknowledging—and treating—the symptoms of collective trauma may often be a necessary prerequisite to healing victims' individual psychic pain: "People who suffer from individual trauma usually have difficulty recovering if the community to which they belong remains shattered" (4).[7]

Yet even as Erikson fleshes out his definition of collective trauma, he begins to feel the presence of some fault lines cutting the phenomenon in two. Indeed, so-called collective traumas affect communities differently depending on their origin. If the cause of the disaster is natural, the damage to the social group is diminished. Indeed, communities that survive a natural disaster often experience a temporary but undeniable sense of joy in the wake of the catastrophe—especially if outsiders aid in healing and reconstruction.[8] Erikson elaborates, citing Anthony F. C. Wallace: "[A] sudden and logically inexplicable wave of good feeling washes over survivors not long after the event itself. . . . [A]ccording to Wallace, a 'stage of euphoria' quickly follows in most natural disasters as people come to realize that the general community is not dead after all" (*New* 235). Luhrmann makes a similar observation, arguing that those who survive "acts of God" seldom feel so strongly that their communities have disintegrated: "When there is a tornado, or an epidemic, or a flood, there is usually no 'we-ness' to the loss. . . . There is not a sense that 'our people' have let us down, that it is a genetic weakness of our flesh or an inadequacy of the way 'we' live. When a flood wiped out North Dakota farming communities, nobody did it to 'us'" (185).

But something different happens when members of the traumatized community believe that other people are culpable for their pain and suffering. Erikson writes, "[D]isasters that are thought to have been brought about by other human beings . . . not only hurt in special ways but bring in their wake feelings of injury and vulnerability from which it is difficult to recover" (*New* 237). The author develops this claim in his discussion of the community of East Swallow. That neighborhood is thrown into peril when major gasoline leaks from nearby underground tanks seep beneath homes, releasing gas clouds that risk residents' health, safety, and sense of security. And when the corporation that owns the tanks hires a team of lawyers in an attempt to avoid liability, the residents of East Swallow feel assaulted again. Though Erikson's thinking on this topic is somewhat preliminary, he nonetheless suggests that a primary effect of this second type of collective trauma is the survivors' loss of trust—both in each other and in the social institutions on which they previously relied:

> The mortar bonding human communities together is made up at least in part of trust and respect and decency and, in moments of crisis, of charity and concern. It is profoundly disturbing to people when these expectations are not met, no matter how well protected they thought they were by that outer crust of cynicism our century seems to have developed in us all. They have already been made vulnerable by a sharp trick of fate, and now they must face the future without those layers of emotional insulation that only a trusted communal surround can provide. That's hard. But the real problem in the long run is that the inhumanity people experience comes to be seen as a natural feature of human life rather than the bad manners of a particular corporation. They think their eyes are being opened to a larger and profoundly unsettling truth: that human institutions cannot be relied on. (239)

When a community suffers a trauma of others' making—especially if those responsible seek to evade or deny responsibility—their pain is compounded by the pervasive sense that they can no longer trust anyone.

Robben identifies the loss of basic trust as one of the primary effects of Argentina's Dirty War—an act of collective violence inflicted on the people by their own government in the late 1970s and early 1980s. During that time, the ruling party oversaw a reign of terror that involved the "disappearance" of as many as thirty thousand suspected enemies of the state. When supposed dissidents were "disappeared," government hit squads would often invade homes when the families living there were most vulnerable. Argentine leaders intended these incursions to disrupt both domestic peace and family security: "The disappearances carried out in the intimacy of the home invaded the primary object-relation of parent and child, and provoked intense guilt feelings among the surviving parents about having failed to protect their adult and adolescent children" (71). Robben draws on the work of the pioneering child psychologist Erik Erikson to make the claim that these primary trust relationships are the foundation on which society is built. Therefore, in disrupting the basic trust that exists among family members, perpetrators disrupt society more broadly considered. Robben goes on to write, "The basic trust of a person is assaulted as much as the integrity of the body, and primary relations are damaged together with the symbolic order of society" (74–75). Thus, the violence done during the Dirty War is not merely physical or psychological; it is "socio-cultural" (75).

Here, I would like to argue that the language of moral injury might help us make clearer the distinction that Kai Erikson, Luhrmann, and Robben are probing. Indeed, there is a more appropriate name for these human-caused collective traumas: collective moral injury. These authors provide preliminary but persuasive evidence that ethical breaches—be they ill-handled gas leaks in East Swallow or government-sponsored kidnappings in

Argentina—inflict a unique type of damage on communities in addition to any harm they might do to individuals.

We see signs of this type of damage—of what I'm calling collective moral injury—in *The Fall*. Indeed, a number of crucial passages attest to the idea that Clamence believes he shares his malady with his generation. The most crucial of these passages is the book's first words—its epigraph drawn from Lermontov's *A Hero of Our Time*. Here is that section in its entirety:

> Some were dreadfully insulted, and quite seriously, to have held up as a model such an immoral character as *A Hero of Our Time*; others shrewdly noticed that the author had portrayed himself and his acquaintances. . . . *A Hero of Our Time*, gentlemen, is in fact a portrait, but not of an individual; it is the aggregate of the vices of our whole generation in their fullest expression. (n.p.)

The message here is clear: Clamence—like Lermontov's hero—is not a unique specimen but a type, a representative sample of the midcentury European. Camus himself coyly says as much in his own description of the book: Clamence "looks at himself in a mirror, but finally pushes it towards others. Where does he stop confessing and start accusing others? Is the narrator putting himself on trial, or his era? Does he represent a specific case, or is he the man of the hour?" (quoted in Todd 342) Clamence seems to say the same thing, suggesting early in his monologue that "all Europe is in the same boat" (Camus 6). If that is true, then perhaps it is productive to speak of the European community after the wars, after the bombs, after the concentration camps as suffering from collective moral injury. And just as Clamence does too little to aid the drowning woman, so too did millions of citizens of France, Britain, Spain, and the rest not risk enough in trying to save the millions of others who perished.

Indeed, Clamence's description of his generation—and of his social group more narrowly speaking—bears out the suggestion. Recall that for Kai Erikson and Robben, the prime symptom of collective moral injury (or what Erikson thinks of as human-caused collective trauma) is the loss of trust. Often, when Clamence describes the society in which he lives, he characterizes it primarily as lacking trust. The absence of this feeling is actually the theme with which Camus opens the novel. After introducing Clamence and his unnamed interlocutor, Camus brings onstage the bartender at the tavern called the Mexico City. Describing him, Clamence says, "[H]e has adopted a distrustful disposition. Whence that look of touchy dignity as if he at least suspected that all is not perfect among men. . . . Mind you, I am not judging him. I consider his distrust justified and should be inclined to share it" (4–5). So not only is his distrust unobjectionable; it is perhaps even advisable.

Furthermore, just a few pages later, Clamence links that distrust to one of the great crimes of World War II: the liquidation of Amsterdam's Jewish Quarter, whose population Clamence pegs at seventy-five thousand. Clamence now lives in the Jewish Quarter; he notes, "I am living on the site of one of the greatest crimes in history. Perhaps that's what helps me to understand the ape and his distrust" (11). The generation of Europeans who witness (and fail to stop) this crime cannot help but be damaged by it, and a theory of collective moral injury helps us understand why distrust is the logical outcome. Soon after that, Clamence pushes the theme further, arguing that Amsterdam is like "the last circle" of hell (14). And as Dante teaches us, the last circle of hell is for the traitors, those who break trust. Living among those he considers traitors, Clamence comes to reconsider his relationships with other people, at one point describing them as "enemies" (79). Elsewhere, he says, "I have no more friends. . . . I have nothing but accomplices" (73).

And, of course, by definition, accomplices are those who are drawn together not by trust but only by mutually assured conviction.

In closing, I want to make it clear that reframing *The Fall* as a moral injury novel does not mean that it is no longer relevant to discussions of trauma. Indeed, perhaps the opposite is true. For while Felman's suggestion that Clamence is traumatized is dubious, she is absolutely right to identify him as a failed witness. Rather, my sense is that in discussing the character's moral injury, we get a better sense of the forces that cause him to fail. Let me be clear: Clamence does not fail because he is ignorant or dismissive of the powerful positive role that witness can play. As a matter of fact, he promulgates a thoroughly compelling image of what witness might actually look like—the powerful vision of sleeping on the floor:

> You see, I've heard of a man whose friend had been imprisoned and who slept on the floor of his room every night in order not to enjoy a comfort of which his friend had been deprived. Who, *cher monsieur*, will sleep on the floor for us? Whether I am capable of it myself? Look, I'd like to be and I shall be. Yes, we shall all be capable of it one day, and that will be salvation. But it's not easy. . . . (32)

And yet in the final pages of the novel, Clamence is not on the floor; he is in bed. And he's in bed because *he is sick*. His illness is a perfect symbol for the moral injury he is suffering. If he were healed of his sickness, he could sleep on the floor. And if he were treated for his moral injury, he could be an effective witness. And that, perhaps, would be salvation.

Notes

1. For an extended discussion of the problematic relationship between trauma theory and the trope of "unspeakability," see my own 2014 essay, "Speak, Trauma: Toward a Revised Understanding of Literary Trauma Theory."

2. Indeed, LaCapra argues that Felman's characterization of Clamence as a "victim of a traumatic incident" is either misleading or warped to fit her thesis (*History* 85). By contrast, he argues that the text should "be read more pointedly as a critique of the position of the bystander, a position that Clamence occupies when he fails to come to the assistance of the woman who falls into the Seine" (76). The claim is persuasive. Yet in what follows, I push past LaCapra in two crucial ways. First, while LaCapra characterizes Clamence as something other than a "victim," he never shakes trauma as a framework for understanding the protagonist's decision, calling the night on the bridge "a traumatic turning point in his life" (81). I argue here that Camus's antihero is not traumatized at all; he is morally injured. Further, LaCapra hedges when describing the woman's actions on the bridge, making much of the fact that she may or may not be a suicide: "[S]he may have jumped, she may have fallen, or something else may have happened" (78n). LaCapra is right to point out the ambiguous nature of the woman's fall. However, he downplays the importance of the sound that immediately follows the fall—a repeated cry. My sense is that the cry is more important than the nature of the fall, insofar as it calls Clamence into a relationship of responsibility with the woman. And the fact that he denies this responsibility leads to his subsequent pain.

3. By my perhaps imperfect count, *nous* appears 59 times in the first half of the novel and 102 times in the second.

4. Again, a rough count has Clamence utter some form of *je* 570 times before the fall; after, the number is 605.

5. He extends his thinking on such themes in a 1994 volume, *A New Species of Trouble*, in which he finds evidence of collective trauma in a variety of other case studies. In that book, he argues more definitively that trauma "has a social dimension" (231). He also writes, "I have been using the term 'trauma' throughout these pages to refer not only to the psychological condition of the people one encounters in those scenes but also to the social texture of the scenes themselves, and that is departure enough from normal usage for me to consider for a moment how 'trauma' can serve as a broad social concept as well as a more narrowly clinical one" (228).

6. He continues, "The collective trauma works its way slowly and even insidiously into the awareness of those who suffer from it, so it does not have the quality of suddenness normally associated with 'trauma.' But it is a form of shock all the same, a gradual realization that the community no longer exists as an effective source of support and that an important part of the self has disappeared. . . . 'I' continue to exist, though damaged and maybe even permanently changed. 'You' continue to exist, though distant and hard to relate to. But 'we' no longer exist as a connected pair or as linked cells in a larger communal body" (Erikson, "Notes" 460).

7. For more on collective trauma, its effects, and its clinical applications, see Audergon, de Jong and Reis, Karenian et al., Nelson, and Vertzberger.

8. Further, Erikson's critics note that events (like natural disasters) should not be understood as intrinsically traumatizing. Notably, Jeffrey Alexander suggests that such approaches succumb to what he calls the "naturalistic fallacy." He counters, "Events are not inherently traumatic. Trauma is a socially mediated attribution. The attribution may be made in real time, as an event unfolds; it may also be made before the event occurs, as an adumbration, or after the event has concluded, as a post-hoc reconstruction. Sometimes, in fact, events that are deeply traumatizing may not have actually occurred at all" (Alexander et al. 8).

5

"Signature Wound"

MORAL INJURY IN IRAQ WAR LITERATURE

The story of Colonel Theodore Westhusing illustrates some of the most crucial dynamics of the moral injury epidemic that played out in the military during the height of the wars in Afghanistan and Iraq. Westhusing graduated third in his class from West Point in 1983, having served as that institution's honor captain during his senior year. After graduation, he became an infantry platoon leader and spent time in Italy, South Korea, and Honduras before rising to the rank of division operations officer at Fort Bragg. Yet he was an academic at heart, and in 2000 he began graduate training in philosophy at Emory University (his dissertation focused on the concept of honor) and later returned to West Point to teach. In the early years of the new millennium, he had become one of the most respected scholars in the field of military ethics. And by all accounts, he lived what he taught, leading what friends and family often characterized as an exemplary moral life. A devout Catholic, a devoted father, and a dedicated teacher, he was generally seen as an exceedingly decent human being.

He was also a staunch defender of the conflicts in Afghanistan and Iraq, believing them to be just wars in the classical definition. So when a former commander asked him to return to active duty in Iraq, he eagerly accepted, believing not only that he could contribute to a worthy cause but also that his service would make him a better teacher. Westhusing was assigned the job of overseeing a private security company with $79 million in contracts to train the Iraqi police force. Early on, his tour was everything he hoped it would be: meaningful, affirming, and active. But he quickly came to be distraught by the bloat and graft that characterized the government's interactions with the contractors it hired. His distress came to a head when he received an anonymous complaint detailing the misdeeds of his contractor. These included allegations of fraud and corruption. At the same time, charges surfaced suggesting that the contractor's employees had either murdered or witnessed the murder of Iraqi civilians. Devastated, Westhusing spiraled into despair. He stopped taking care of himself, and his emails to his family took on darker tones. Then, on June 5, 2005, Westhusing was found dead in his quarters, the victim of an apparently self-inflicted gunshot wound to the head. He left a suicide note:

> Thanks for telling me it was a good day until I briefed you. [Redacted name]—You are only interested in your career and provide no support to your staff—no msn [mission] support and you don't care. I cannot support a msn that leads to corruption, human right abuses and liars. I am sullied—no more. I didn't volunteer to support corrupt, money grubbing contractors, nor work for commanders only interested in themselves. I came to serve honorably and feel dishonored. I trust no Iraqi. I cannot live this way. All my love to my family, my wife and my precious children. I love you and trust you only. Death before being dishonored any more. Trust is essential—I don't know who trust [sic] anymore. Why serve when you cannot accomplish the mission, when you no longer believe in the cause, when your every effort and breath to succeed meets with lies, lack of support, and

selfishness? No more. Reevaluate yourselves, cdrs [commanders].
You are not what you think you are and I know it.
    COL Ted Westhusing
    Life needs trust. Trust is no more for me here in Iraq. (Miller)

At the time of his death, Westhusing was the highest-ranking member of the US Armed Forces to die in Iraq.

With the benefit of hindsight, it seems quite likely that Westhusing was suffering from moral injury. His witnessing of ethical breaches—by both contractors and his superiors—left him feeling deeply betrayed, and that sense of betrayal sent him down a path of isolation and poor self-care that ultimately ended in his suicide. But it is not the mere presence of moral injury symptoms that makes Westhusing's story instructive. In this, as previous chapters have made clear, he is far from alone. Recall that David Wood dubs moral injury the "signature wound" of the US wars in Afghanistan and Iraq (hereafter Operation Enduring Freedom and Operation Iraqi Freedom, or OEF/OIF), and recall also that it is the study of their veterans' psychic suffering that gives rise to the moral injury category. No, Westhusing's story is interesting for two other reasons that will loom large in this chapter. First, moral injury hit him so hard because he was a deeply moral person to begin with. He was both invested in and a scholar of the military virtues of honor, duty, and justice, and by all accounts, he took them as a personal code. Thus, seeing his brothers and sisters in arms breaching this code was exceedingly destabilizing. Second, Westhusing seemed almost totally ignorant of the moral landscape of Iraq before he arrived. He was a faithful advocate of these missions before he saw them up close. Westhusing's ignorance is indicative of the yawning gap between the battlefield and the home front in these most recent of American wars. As many have noted, the American public has been able to largely ignore the bloody battles being fought in their name, and this lack of awareness has spared them some of the moral pain they perhaps should feel.

In this chapter, we turn to the now-burgeoning literature of the wars in Afghanistan and Iraq in an effort to identify the presence of moral injury in these texts. If moral injury is the signature wound of OEF and OIF, one would expect to find it in the books, stories, and poems they have inspired. Indeed, we do. (As the bulk of recent American war fiction has focused on the conflict in Iraq, most of the following analysis engages works set there.) However, this chapter pursues a subthesis regarding the cause of veterans' moral injury. The books and poems feature depictions of wartime events that have come to be understood as hallmark triggers of MI: the inadvertent killing of civilians, the death of children, the handling of human remains, and the witnessing of superiors' bad behavior. But a sustained close reading of OEF/OIF literature reveals a less obvious cause of moral injury: the ignorance of those who remain on the home front—or, the painful fact that more civilians are not similarly injured. Peter Yeomans and Chris Antal, specialists with experience counseling morally injured veterans, suggest that this idea comes up frequently in their clinical work. MI, they argue, "is as much about society's avoidance and denial as it is about the ethical burdens that veterans bear" (Press). This notion animates much recent war fiction, and the military characters we see are often anguished by the fact that they carry the burden of moral injury alone. This realization increases their sense of isolation and enhances their pain.

But before we turn our attention to the ignorance of civilians, we must first explain why moral injury is so widespread among OEF/OIF veterans. We touched upon two reasons in the introduction: the nature of guerrilla/counterinsurgency campaigns and the implementation of reflexive-fire training in the second half of the twentieth century. Like the Vietnam War, both OEF and OIF are primarily guerrilla wars in which US service members battle small bands of combatants who blend in with local populations. Insofar as it is difficult to distinguish between enemy fighters and civilians, US service members are forced to make impossible choices when engaging the enemy. Given that these service members are trained to fire reflexively, they sometimes are responsible for civilian deaths. Yet the proliferation of moral injury in OEF and OIF not only springs from their "immoral" acts; it is also caused by the extraordinary moral quality of those who fight our wars.

In *Adaptive Disclosure*, Litz et al. speak of the "warrior ethos"— the general mindset of American enlistees. Crucial to this ethos is a heightened sense of moral purpose: "Warriors tend to have highly developed moral identities and seek every opportunity, on duty or off, to champion their moral values. . . . Warriors always pledge themselves not only to uphold an explicit code of conduct to the best of their ability, but also to protect the social order and promote its highest development" (37–38). It is impossible to be morally injured if one doesn't have a well-defined moral code. Litz et al. argue that by contrast, US service members often have a *heightened* sense of morality. They see themselves as called to a higher purpose, putting their lives on the line for a cause that is bigger than they are.[1] As one character in Phil Klay's short story "Psychological Operations" puts it, "[Y]ou do feel better than most people. You risked your life for something bigger than yourself. How many people can say that? You chose to serve" (203). Thus, those who serve may be more likely to suffer the effects of moral injury. Yet the proliferation of moral injury in OEF and OIF isn't due only to the qualities and actions of the service members. Forces outside their control conspire to make their circumstances increasingly morally injurious. First among them is the remarkable duration of both conflicts; each ranks among the longest wars in US history. Their length has inspired DeRosa and Peebles to suggest that the "wars in Afghanistan and Iraq exist in perpetuity" (208).

The length of these conflicts—combined with the US government's decision to rely solely on a volunteer force—has required military commanders to force service members to undergo multiple tours, often in quick succession, and this much time in country exerts remarkable stress. Further, the shifting nature of these "perpetual" wars has forced leadership to change strategies over time. Such changes lead to frequently shifting rules of engagement, which leave service members unsure about acceptable tactics, strategies, and—most importantly—targets. As Wood writes, "In the collision between the [shifting] official rules and the reality of war, moral injury was widespread" (*What* 195). But the changing nature of these conflicts has long been apparent on both the micro and the macro levels, and service members are sometimes disillusioned by the seeming absence of a stable mission. (This absence was especially troubling in Iraq after US forces failed to find the weapons of mass destruction that were the nominal *casus belli*.) Are these antiterrorism projects? Nation-building efforts? Are they attempts to bolster and defend new democracies? Wars to topple oppressive regimes? Are they purely humanitarian efforts?

For many troops, the absence of clear answers to these questions makes the violence seem at best senseless and at worst murderous. To this point, Wood cites the experience of the Iraq veteran (and military chaplain) Steve Dundas. For him, traveling in Iraq

> was devastating: young Americans gruesomely injured or dying; villages and towns turned to rubble; streams of refugees; the few who ventured out to the market or mosque risking being maimed by suicide bombs. And by that time, the rationale for the 2003 U.S.

invasion of Iraq had been exposed, Dundas realized, as a fabrica-
tion. It all struck him like a physical blow. "I felt lied to. And I felt
those lies cost too many thousands of American lives and far too
much destruction," Dundas told me over a couple of beers one
sunny afternoon in Virginia Beach. What he had seen from afar
as a righteous intervention to unseat a barbaric dictator and bring
democracy to Iraq's people now appeared as one of the most in-
credibly disastrous foreign policy things we ever got involved in.
(*What* 213–14)

Dundas is not alone, and as mentioned previously, service members' perception of their leaders' duplicity is a signal trigger of MI.
Taken together, this collection of effects forms a uniquely toxic
stew—one that has spurred widespread moral injury.[2]

We see evidence of moral injury's extended reach first and foremost in the number of OEF/OIF veterans looking for care after
their service. Brancu et al. note that of the 1.2 million veterans who
had sought VA care as of 2015, 57.6 percent had received a mental
health diagnosis (2). And while specialists haven't settled on a met-
ric for identifying which portion of this group is morally injured,
most believe it is large. Not surprisingly, then, moral injury features
prominently in OEF/OIF novels, stories, and poems. During the
first decade or so of the wars in Afghanistan and Iraq, there was a
popular belief that the wars had yet to produce literary works of
any real significance. In a 2012 review of Iraq War art, Roger Luckhurst claims that "[n]o defining literary texts have emerged from
the overlapping contexts of the invasion, the Iraqi civil war, or the
occupation" ("War Times" 713). That perception has changed significantly since, and we now have an embarrassment of OEF/OIF
texts, many of which have won or been nominated for major prizes.

In the following, I focus on the work of four Iraq War veterans:
Brian Turner's poetry (especially in *Here, Bullet*), Kevin Powers's

The Yellow Birds, Phil Klay's *Redeployment*, and Roy Scranton's *War Porn*. I choose these texts not to help expand or reify any sort of new war canon, but simply because they have been widely and positively reviewed, because they have received the lion's share of early critical attention from scholars in the field, and because their authors' experience in country gives them an intimate view of the psychological hazards of contemporary military action.

We should say at the outset that none of the literary works addressed in this chapter mention moral injury by name. Brett Litz and his team wouldn't publish their pioneering essay on the concept for another four years when Turner put out *Here, Bullet* in 2005—the same year Scranton began writing *War Porn*. And the books by Klay and Powers appeared before Litz et al.'s contemporary definition of moral injury was even five years old. Yet even if the service members and veterans in these books didn't have access to the term, evidence of the harm MI causes is everywhere.

The military characters in these works are psychologically savvy, and they have a basic awareness of the language of trauma. The chaplain in Phil Klay's short story "Prayer in the Furnace," talking with a troubled service member in his unit, reviews the young man's symptoms and thinks, "It was a pretty complete PTSD checklist" (148). The veteran Aaron in *War Porn* is so acquainted with that checklist that his response to trauma is ironic. Told that he has a "pretty negative worldview," he responds casually, "Yeah, well, I'm all traumatized and shit" (Scranton, *War* 29). Indeed, some characters are so familiar with trauma in the post-Vietnam era that they welcome it as part of the war experience. One of the unnamed narrators in Scranton's novel describes his unit as seeking out PTSD as a badge of honor: "*We expected nothing less than shell shock and trauma, we lusted for thousand-yard stares—lifelong connoisseurs of hallucinatory violence, we already knew everything, felt everything"* (*War* 54).[3]

The ubiquity of trauma notwithstanding, it's clear that something else is going on in Afghanistan and Iraq—something for which even these hardened recruits are not prepared—and that service members are experiencing a brand of psychic suffering that escapes the PTSD paradigm. Scranton provides an effective image of it in his description of a catch-all mental health tent on the ground in Iraq:

> A guy in Bravo Battery named Pizza had started walking around naked. When he got up one afternoon and pissed all over the floor, he was put on suicide watch. He screamed into the night, eerie piercing howls of terror. Villaguerrero punched some dude from Alpha, got his rank taken away, and was tasked to DIVARTY. Bullwinkle crashed a hemmet into the compound's main gate, tearing open a fuel tank and spilling gas everywhere. Lieutenant Krauss had started talking to himself. (*War* 106)

Scranton's narrator says the tent holds roughly two hundred troops, and he describes it as "bedlam" (106). This word is as arcane as it is telling, evoking a time when mental illness was poorly understood and haphazardly treated—and when the nature and source of our psychic pains were unclear. (Of course, many of the troops' symptoms are closely associated with moral injury.) Yet this is "bedlam" for today, housing service members whose suffering specialists can't ignore even if they can't quite identify it. On a similar note, Jenks, one of the protagonists in Klay's "War Stories," speaks briefly to the distinction between what we know and what we don't know about service members' pain; to wit, he knows that he carries psychic baggage from his service but is also quite aware that it's not related to PTSD symptoms. Asked if he is traumatized, he responds quickly, "No. . . . Explosions don't startle me. I'm all good" (227).[4] And in *War Porn*, when Aaron's girlfriend is asked if he has PTSD, she says no but nonetheless admits that "something happened" to him (308).

As one reads on, it becomes apparent that this "something" originates in the precarious ethical landscape of Afghanistan and Iraq—which one of Klay's commanders calls a "morally bruising battlefield" (145). Further, it seems to come not from what the troops *survive* but what they *do*. Numerous characters describe a pain associated with not being able to reverse a bad act. As Aaron puts it in *War Porn*, "Once you make a decision, once you do something, you can't take it back. . . . You don't get to say 'Oh, wait, what I did was wrong, so now I want to get someone else in trouble so I can feel better.' If it was wrong, it was wrong. But I did it. Nothing can change that" (Scranton, *War* 315). Bartle says something similar in *The Yellow Birds*: "[T]here isn't any making up for killing women or even watching women get killed, or for that matter killing men and shooting them in the back and shooting them more times than necessary to actually kill them and it was like just trying to kill everything you saw" (K. Powers 144). Bartle also realizes that his reaction to these acts is somehow outside the pale of normal experience. Guilt and shame are standard human emotions; what he feels is different: "Anyone can feel shame. I remember myself, sitting under neglected and overgrown brush, afraid of nothing in the world more than having to show myself for what I had become" (132).

It is telling, then, that Powers selects as his novel's epigraph a quote from the seventeenth-century author and physician Sir Thomas Browne about the resilient mind's ability to move past misdeeds: "To be ignorant of evils to come, and forgetfull of evils past, is a mercifull provision in nature, whereby we digest the mixture of our few and evil dayes, and our delivered senses not relapsing into cutting remembrances, our sorrows are not kept raw by the edge of repetitions." In the novel's milieu, however, the quote is aspirational, as neither Bartle nor his friend Murph are able to forget their "evils past"; both are tortured by "cutting re-membrances" of their and others' misdeeds, and their sorrows *do* remain raw from repetition. The state of mind Browne describes is effectively the mirror opposite of moral injury, and Powers and the rest are working to develop a creative language that describes MI's effects on US troops.

Powers, Klay, Scranton, and Turner portray the contemporary battlefield as rife with MIEs, or morally injurious events. And while their depiction of veterans is sympathetic, it is decidedly not flattering. Their protagonists both witness and perpetrate a dizzying number of bad acts. Powers's *The Yellow Birds* tells the story of two young service members, Bartle and Murph, and the many psychic trials they undergo in Iraq. (Bartle is ground down by those trials, and Murph cracks and effectively commits suicide.) They are led by a commanding officer named Sterling who is both ruthlessly effective and guilty of war crimes. I would contend that both Bartle and Murph are morally injured, but it is impossible to identify which of the many unspeakable events they experience causes their suffering. In the first couple dozen pages of *The Yellow Birds*, after an intense firefight, service members train their guns on an oncoming car with white sheets billowing out the back win-dows, and Sterling opens fire without verifying that its passengers are a threat. It turns out they are an elderly civilian couple who die almost instantly. Seeing the display, Murph mutters, "Holy shit, that bitch got murdered" (22). At other points, the pair is caught up in firefights in which they kill Iraqi fighters who are little more than children. And when Murph goes missing after a mortar attack on their compound, Bartle and Sterling enlist the help of a local peddler in the search for him. Finding Murph's desecrated body, they drop it in a river rather than trying to repatriate his desecrated remains; Sterling subsequently murders the peddler (211). Then Powers implies that unit members lay waste to a local village, killing indiscriminately: "The city would be covered with brass casings. Battered buildings would have new holes. Blood would be swept into the streets and washed into gutters before we were through" (204). Clinicians could make a compelling case that any one of these events is an MIE.

Phil Klay's *Redeployment* is a short story collection that features a similar variety of horrors scattered throughout a dozen tales of veterans returning from Iraq and Afghanistan. The title piece has a handful of Marines killing an unarmed insurgent hiding in a drainage ditch: "About four or five Marines aimed straight down, fired into the shit. Except me. . . . [S]omething in me is going to break if I do this" (15). The collection also features a number of examples of what specialists refer to as betrayal-based MIEs—in which the injurious act is the misdeed of a commanding officer. As just one example, the speaker in "Unless It's a Sucking Chest Wound" mentions one of his commanders, a Lieutenant Colonel Motes, an "incompetent asshole whose poor grasp of COIN [counterinsurgency] was getting them hurt" (261). But the most sustained sequence of MIEs comes in the story "Prayer in the Furnace," in which a service member named Rodriguez tries to talk to a military chaplain about atrocities committed by members of his unit. A commanding officer refers to them as a "kill company" (145), and they are responsible for heinous acts. Early on in the story, company members, on bad intel from incompetent commanders, fire a rocket-propelled grenade that kills a group of children (135). This is an extremely unfortunate accident, but

Rodriguez also speaks more vaguely of killing "somebody you're not supposed to" (139)—an indication that some of his fellow service members' bad kills are intentional. Indeed, at the end of the story, another service member named Newberry testifies that he and his unit are guilty of the abuse, torture, and murder of innocent civilians (161). He even has digital photographs to prove it.

Aaron, one of the main characters in *War Porn*, also has a flash drive of digital evidence of service members' crimes. The book has a number of plot strands: bookend sections focus on Aaron's tortured return from Iraq,[5] and sandwiched between these are two longer narratives. The first is a semiautobiographical account of a soldier named Wilson's time on the ground in Iraq, and the second, housed within the first, tells the story of Qasim, an Iraqi graduate student trying to ride out the US invasion. (Interspersed among these sections are pieces of modernist-inspired poetry grouped under the subheading "Babylon.") The Wilson sections include a number of striking MIEs. Early on, Wilson—who often serves as a driver—is told to run over civilian boys if they get in the way of the military caravan: "'[I]f they don't get out of the way, run him over. I mean it. Run him over.' . . . I imagined the Iraqi boy's body dragged beneath the humvee's tires, three tons of steel rolling over his chest, squirting intestines onto the road" (47). Later on, Wilson witnesses the killing of an unarmed woman (83). And in one of the narrative's more stomach-churning episodes, a service member named Nash shoots in the chest a mentally handicapped boy who is lofting rocks at an American tank. His commander's callous remarks in praising Nash only render the episode more disgusting: "The only thing Nash did wrong was forget his training. . . . *two* rounds center mass! Maybe next time you'll get it right!" (265).

Yet all of this is a prelude to the novel's conclusion, in which Aaron shows photographs of prisoner abuse to a civilian named Matt.

The collection of images documents a panoply of pain and violence: beatings, stress positions, degradation, and death (310–22). One of the more disturbing photos features a "close-up head-and-shoulders of a mangled, bloody face" (318). Matt asks Aaron if they killed the man; he replies, "Fuck no. We just stressed him to the point where his body failed" (318)—a macabre distinction without a difference. The most poignant revelation in this photo sequence is that Aaron's company captures, abuses, debases, and tortures Qasim, who by this point in the novel is a fully realized, thoroughly sympathetic character. It should also be noted that most the atrocities described above are enabled by the characters' consistent dehumanization of Iraqis, who are usually small, flat characters whom the troops frequently refer to as "hajjis." Such widespread dehumanization of other people might trigger moral injury on its own.

We also should not ignore the fact that for some, the mere act of killing—even a "good" kill in a wartime scenario—is an MIE. As the narrator of "Redeployment" succinctly puts it, "It's not easy to kill people, either" (Klay 3). Brian Turner seems to take this perspective in *Here, Bullet*. In a short poem entitled "Sadiq," he writes,

> It should make you shake and sweat,
> nightmare you, strand you in a desert
> of irrevocable desolation, the consequences
> seared into the vein, no matter what adrenaline
> feeds the muscle its courage, no matter
> what god shines down on you, no matter
> what crackling pain and anger
> you carry in your fists, my friend,
> it should break your heart to kill. (56)

The poem builds dramatic tension by obscuring the referent of its opening pronoun, "It," until the very last word. Thus do we learn about killing's effects before we are introduced to the concept it-self. In forcing us to meditate on the results of killing, Turner re-invests the tired cliché "break your heart" with new power, and also asks that we think of killing not only as the end of a victim's story but as the beginning of a dark new chapter for the person who pulls the trigger. Turner's speaker is clearly haunted by the death he or she caused, even though there is little indication ei-ther in "Sadiq" or elsewhere in *Here, Bullet* that it breached either standing rules of engagement or battlefield morality. Regardless, he or she exhibits one of the trademark symptoms of moral injury: isolation. Yes, killing makes the speaker "shake and sweat," but it also "strands you in a desert / of irrevocable desolation." In this, "Sadiq" is like *The Yellow Birds*, *Redeployment*, and *War Porn*, all of which not only depict a wide variety of MIEs but show characters who have MI symptoms.

An exhaustive list of the moral injury symptoms in these works would make up a book in its own right, so we focus here on a few representative examples. Recall one last time that the first major symptom of moral injury is irrational or excessive rage, or, as Turner describes it, the "crackling pain and anger / you carry in your fists." Klay captures the essence of this symptom most effectively—and seems most aware of the danger it poses. In "After Action Report," a service member takes responsibility for a ques-tionable kill that is not his own; the victim is a "kid [who] had grabbed his dad's AK." His fellow service member "shot the kid three times before he hit the ground. Can't miss at that range. The kid's mother ran out to try to pull her son back into the house. She came just in time to see bits of him blow out of his shoul-ders" (32). In the aftermath of this gruesome death, both service members experience moral injury symptoms; both withdraw into themselves and, insofar as it's possible to do so, avoid the company of others. But the narrator also guts his way through inexplicable bouts of anger: "As we moved down the road, my hands jittery with adrenaline, I wanted to scream, '*Fuck!*' as loud as I could, and keep screaming it through the whole convoy until I got to let off a round in someone. I started gripping the sides of the .50. When my hands were white, I would let go. I did that for a half hour, and then the rage left me and I felt exhausted" (51). Klay dwells on this emotion long enough so that the reader can sense the threat the service member now poses to himself and others. We see something similar in the character Rodriguez from "Prayer in the Furnace." His company chaplain notices the service member's seething rage before he even knows his story: "Violent microexpressions periodically flashed across his face, the snarling contortions of an angry dog. . . . [H]is face again turned to violence. . . . I'd never seen a Marine like this, and I didn't really want to be alone with him" (127–28). That "microexpressions" are the subject here, rather than the service member himself, suggests that the rage is difficult for him to control. Further, the chaplain's reaction indicates that such anger makes a person toxic and drives others away. Thus it feeds the second major symptom of moral injury: isolation.

Among the works addressed here, *The Yellow Birds* most poignantly testifies to the ways that moral injury leaves one stranded in Turner's "desert of irrevocable desolation." As Murph falls deeper into his own pain, he separates himself more thoroughly from those who might help him. And this isolation becomes physically dangerous when he wanders off the base into the local scrublands. He is almost immediately captured by insurgents, tortured, maimed, and killed. In the weeks and months that follow Murph's death, Bartle—who feels guilty for promising Murph's mother to look after him—drifts away from his unit and, later, his family. Early on, he takes some comfort in the delusion that his loneliness is "explicable" in terms other than those of his friend's passing: "It felt good, somewhere behind my breastbone, to sense that this separation was explicable, a mere failing of language, and my loneliness could proceed with a different cause for a little while longer" (K. Powers 53).

The idea that his is a sort of causeless, freestanding solitude is comforting to Bartle. But eventually he is forced to accept the fact that his pain is a result of Murph's death. On returning home after his tour, he locks himself in his room for weeks at a time and later rents a studio apartment that allows him to avoid other people entirely. (In *War Porn*, Aaron follows a similar path, wandering the country aimlessly on his motorcycle.) In Klay's "Prayer in the Furnace," a mentoring priest explains the link between wrongdoing and estrangement from others: "Sin is a lonely thing, a worm wrapped around the soul, shielding it from love, from joy, from communion with fellow men and with God. The sense that I am alone, that none can hear me, none can understand, that no one answers my cries, it is a sickness" (156). The man's language is theological, but he speaks of the isolating effects of sin in ways that vividly recall the MI paradigm. Here is sin that isolates, that drives one from community and solace, and that is best understood as a "sickness."

Angry and alone, the service members and veterans in these pieces abandon basic principles of self-care. Often they self-medicate with alcohol: Bartle, Sterling, and Aaron drink heavily, and other characters turn to harder drugs. These habits harm them personally and professionally. A number of characters in *Redeployment* see their relationships with wives and lovers hurt by alcohol use.

And Rodriguez mentions the harm it's done to his professional advancement: "You know, if I hadn't been busted down after that DUI, I'd probably be leading this squad" (Klay 137). As previously mentioned, such poor self-care is often connected to both para-suicidal and suicidal behavior, as Aaron's comments indicate: "The truth is, Matt, I'm gonna burrow like a tick in the skin of the grimiest, nastiest Rust Belt shithole I can find and shoot heroin till I die," he says, with no detectable irony (Scranton, *War* 297). And while Murph's off-base wandering isn't technically suicidal, it might as well be, as the perils of going solo and unarmed in insurgent territory are obvious to all. Like his friend, Bartle flirts with suicide during his months of isolation: "There is a fine line between not wanting to wake up and actually wanting to kill yourself, and while I discovered you can walk that line for a long while without even noticing, anybody who is around you surely will" (K. Powers 135). Bartle is fortunate that a few friends and family members actually do notice that he's walking that line, and he survives through the end of *The Yellow Birds*.

Other characters are not so lucky. In the closing pages of "Prayer in the Furnace," a number of Rodriguez's fellow service members step over the line, and that story of carnage ends with a spate of suicides (Klay 162–66). And Turner's poem "Eulogy" is a verse portrait of one service member who chooses to end his life in the middle of his tour:

It happens on a Monday, at 11:20 a.m.,
as tower guards eat sandwiches
and seagulls drift by on the Tigris river.
Prisoners tilt their heads to the west
though burlap sacks and duct tape blind them.
The sound reverberates down concertina coils
the way piano wire thrums when given slack.
And it happens like this, on a blue day of sun,

when Private Miller pulls the trigger
to take brass and fire into his mouth. (20)

Though the cause of Miller's suicide is not named, the mention of prisoners, bound brutishly with burlap and duct tape, suggests a link between Miller's death and the captive people's mistreatment. Turner uses the same technique here that he uses in "Sadiq": only in the last two lines do we learn that the "It" that opens the poem is a death. This formal mirroring makes "Eulogy" a sort of sequel to "Sadiq" and suggests that the killing that "breaks your heart" in the latter poem might give way to an even more tragic end.

Poor self-care and suicide are in part caused by demoralization, and many characters in Turner, Powers, Klay, and Scranton live on with a dramatically diminished sense of their own worth, defining themselves in terms of the wrongs they have done. In *War Porn*, Aaron puts it bluntly: "We're devils, Matthew. For real. You gotta see things for what they are" (Scranton, *War* 297). Of course, one needn't fall back on religious language—"devils"—to capture that feeling. Past the midway point of *The Yellow Birds*, Bartle explains an almost physical sense of his own guilt: "I was guilty of something, that much was certain, that much I could feel on a cellular level" (K. Powers 179). This notion, that awareness of wrongdoing might lodge in one's cells, sheds new light on the demoralizing power of moral injury. Bartle is using a biological idiom to explain the way that his sins have caused him to reconsider not only his previous actions but his bodily existence. (Dostoevsky's "trichinae" are another example of the biological incarnation of wrongdoing.) So it is not surprising, a bit earlier in the book, to hear him refer to himself as a "kind of cripple" (143).

We could go on. These novels, stories, and poems bear out Litz's and Wood's claims regarding the prevalence of moral injury in the US military after the turn of the millennium. One could make a convincing argument that *most* of the main characters in these texts are morally injured by their service. Accordingly—and un-surprisingly, then—we see the concept's marks on these books' form. Returning for a moment to Aaron's language in the previous paragraph, we might notice that his statement—"We're devils"— is not just a self-description; it's an exaggeration. Certainly he does some diabolical things, but he describes *himself* as diabolical. For morally injured people like Aaron, evil feels as if it is infectious, and infections spread, and they seem to have an exaggerated effect on self and surroundings. It is for this reason that hyperbole is a moral injury trope. It characterizes some of Aaron's other state-ments about the war too. Early in the novel, he speaks not only of himself as totally irredeemable but of the country of Iraq itself as *wholly* past saving: "Iraq's a fucking disaster. The whole thing. Staying's a disaster. Leaving's a disaster. It's a fucking shithole" (Scranton, *War* 29). Here, the entirety of the war effort is doomed, and the fact that neither staying nor leaving is a workable option means that this doom feels perpetual.

Aaron isn't the only veteran who feels as if Iraq is a hellish ham-ster wheel. Bartle sees the war as a film strip spooling on endlessly, ghoulishly: "We'd go back into a city that had fought this battle yearly; a slow, bloody parade in fall to mark the change of season. We'd drive them out. We always had. We'd kill them. They'd shoot us and blow off our limbs and run into the hills and wadis, back into the alleys and dusty villages. Then they'd come back, and we'd start over again" (K. Powers 91). Powers's pronoun selection—in order, we, we, we, we, they, they, we—emphasizes both the rep-etitious quality of the war and the back-and-forth nature of the conflict. This is battle as an eternal ping-pong game. To fight a forever war like this is to feel perpetually threatened, so it comes as no surprise when Klay's Rodriguez describes Iraq as a place where *everybody* is unhinged, dangerous: "People trying to kill you, *everybody* angry, *everybody* crazy all around you, smacking the shit out of people" (Klay 151; emphasis mine). In Iraq, if everyone is angry and everybody is crazy, then there is no place to hide and (seemingly) no way to avoid danger. Bartle and Murph come to see the country this way. Early on, they take comfort in the numbers of US casualties simply because those numbers are ultimately finite. Yet as time passes, that cap seems to lift, and they come to see casualties as innumerable. Bartle eventually admits, "We didn't know the list was limitless" (K. Powers 13).

In "Bodies," Klay makes a similar point in even more hyperbolic terms. The story's main character works in Mortuary Affairs—the group tasked with processing the dead. (As Litz and others point out, handling human remains is a frequent trigger of moral injury in war zones.) As that story unfolds, we learn that some of the protagonist's fellow service members come to see an endless line of corpses behind each body, stretching through space and time: "Midway through deployment, guys started swearing they could feel spirits everywhere. Not just around the bodies, and not just Marine dead. Sunni dead, Shi'a dead, Kurd dead, Christian dead. All the dead of all Iraq, even all the dead of Iraqi history, the Akkadian Empire and the Mongols and the American invasion" (55). Thus do all the deaths in the region for all of time converge on a single morgue, on a single body—a terrifying thought.

That these bodies spill out from all time into the same place only enhances the sublime menace of Iraq. For Powers, its desert doesn't merely house corpses; it produces them: "All others who died in Al Tafar were part of the landscape, as if something had sown seeds in that city that made bodies rise from the earth, in the dirt or up through the pavement like flowers after a frost, dried and withering under a cold, bright sun" (124). In *The Yellow Birds*, corpses are the earth and are produced by the earth; they are both the soil and the plants that spring forth from the soil. Imagery like this suggests that in Powers's novel, the natural world is a terrifying presence—a silent threat whose limbs reach beyond the horizon. Powers writes, "Day after day of staring into the desert stretched out on all sides like an ocean of twice-burned ash. . . . Outside the desert still expanded, slowly chewing foliage up the way a wave breaks on a shore" (183). Here is an image of self-consuming nature, ghoulishly eating itself. And even when the characters look for solace in the sky above, they find none. It seems as if the desert ocean has overcome even the heavens, which Powers refers to as "the universe . . . cast aside and drowned" (125). Once when Bartle looks up on a clear night, the stars seem dead: "I knew that at least a few of the stars I saw were probably gone already, collapsed into nothing. I felt like I was looking at a lie" (48). One is left with the sense that the entire universe—and not merely the surrounding desert—is filled with the desolating sublime.

But where Powers's protagonists sense threat around and above, Turner feels it coming from below. In "Kirkuk Oilfield, 1927," Iraq's oil reserves are no store of dark riches, but rather the flammable blood of a terrible, subterranean god:

> *We live on the roof of Hell*, he says,
> and Ahmed believes it, he's watched the gas flares
> rise from holes in the earth, he's seen the black river
> wash through the village in a flood of oil
> as if the drillers had struck a vein deep in the skull of God, and
> the old man says
> *Boy, you must learn how to live here*—
> where the dead are buried deep in the mind
> of God, manifest in man and woman,
> given to earth in dark blood,
> given to earth in fire. (23)

Here, the natural world is refigured as a terrifying hellscape, and in the last lines of the poem, men and women who die are sacrifices to the cruel, black earth. That this hellscape is managed by a God in whose head—in whose dark blood—the dead are buried only enhances the sense of existential dread.

Of course, one might hope that even in such a darkly sublime universe, solace might be found in our neighbors. Yet that possibility is elusive for Scranton, who also closes his novel beneath the ground: "A dig just across the state line in Colorado had found seven skeletons whose bones showed evidence of defleshing, chopping, marrow extraction, and burning. There'd been a lot of skepticism until a biologist from the University of Colorado tested fossilized human feces at the site for myoglobin, a protein found in human muscle" (*War* 327). Humans, it seems, have been at each other's throats since time immemorial; they are both residents and products of a violent cosmos.

The menace of the universe—along with the menace of our neighbor—renders the morally injured person's isolation even more piercing. And as suggested earlier, this isolation manifests itself in text in terms of signs of solitude, symbolic and grammatical markers of aloneness. We see the most dramatic proliferation of signs of solitude in *The Yellow Birds*. They accumulate near the novel's climax, the discovery of Murph's corpse. Accordingly, the minaret from which Murph is thrown sits eerily apart from the surrounding settlements: "It jutted out precariously over the bank of the river, a protuberance of mottled stone. There was nothing between us and the tower but a road and barren fields" (201). Matching the minaret is a single tree, similarly set off from other vegetation: "On the side of the road a tree rose out of the otherwise sterile field, bent and swaying softly in the stale breeze" (202). Like these lone landmarks, Murph by this point is cut off from community, and Bartle and Sterling imagine the boy split from the roster of US troops: "We had looked for him hard, *this one boy, this one name* and number on a list" (204; emphasis mine). Again, repetition—this one boy, this one name, the one number—confirms ways in which Bartle has broken away from the sea of other numbers, other boys. When they do find him, instead of returning Murph's body to his family, or to an American graveyard, they release him into a river that joins with the Tigris.

With a lonely image, Powers emphasizes the fact that Sterling and Bartle ensure Murph's isolation as he decomposes: "And I saw his body finally break apart near the mouth of the gulf, where the shadows of the date palms fell in long, dark curtains on his bones, now scattered, and swept them out to sea, toward a line of waves that break forever as he enters them" (226). The dumping of the corpse haunts Bartle and leads to his own solitude, and Powers makes grammatical decisions that emphasize that estrangement. As in other literature engaging MI themes, in the moments of Bartle's most acute suffering, the first-person "I" features prominently. As just one example, here is an extended passage describing a walk Bartle takes during a brief leave in Germany after disposing of Murph:

> *I* walked outside onto the cobblestone streets looking down at my feet. *I* am sure people noticed me, as *I* thought *I* heard a few gasps while *I* walked, but *I* never looked up. It wasn't in *me*. My separation was complete. *I* walked aimlessly until *I* saw lamplight falling softly through the red curtains of a building near the outskirts of town. *I* heard music and women's voices coming through the thin openings above the windowsill. *I* hadn't particularly been looking for this place, but *I* remembered a cav scout in Al Tafar writing down the address for me. (61; emphasis mine).

With his grammatical decisions, Powers emphasizes the "completeness" of Bartle's separation. He returns to this technique a few dozen pages later as Bartle sits in an aircraft soaring high above the

US mainland. As he drifts off to sleep, he thinks, "I want to go . . . I want to . . . I want . . . I" (102). With each iteration of the brief phrase, Powers breaks off one word until only "I" remains. Here, Powers dramatizes the way that moral injury peels surrounding figures away from the self, leaving it ultimately alone.

In an early passage in the novel, we learn that Bartle is aware that his service has narrowed his field of vision: "I'd been trained to think war was the great unifier," he says, "that it brought people closer together than any other activity on earth. Bullshit. War is the great maker of solipsists" (12). A number of writers have begun to critique the "solipsistic" feel of both *The Yellow Birds* and other major Iraq War fiction. In a *Harper's* review essay of contemporary war fiction, tellingly titled "First-Person Shooters," Sam Sacks observes that many recent Afghanistan and Iraq novels "share a consistent perspective. They view the war from the restricted point of view of individual characters, to whom no larger picture of the conflict is visible."[6] For Sacks, the absence of this "larger picture" is a flaw that allows readers to become complacent and avoid asking tough questions about these wars: "Why did we fight these wars, and what were we trying to achieve? Did we succeed or did we fail? What consequences have we wrought on the countries we attacked? What, if anything, have we learned?"

Adrian Lewis makes similar comments about OEF/OIF war writing and suggests that the narrowness of perspective results from the current popularity of the "embedding" model of war reporting, in which a journalist travels with a group of service members in hopes of providing a ground's-eye-view account of battle. Because of the popularity of embedding, much war writing, Lewis argues, suffers from a "tunnel vision effect" that gives readers a "tactical picture" while depriving them of the wider "strategic" view (quoted in Deer 316). Finally, Scranton himself, critiquing other authors' war writing, sees this narrow focus on both the "tactical" details of combat and the attendant psychic pain of veterans as dangerous. He sees that focus as related to our overreliance on the myth of the "trauma hero" and argues that "by focusing so insistently on the psychological trauma American soldiers have had to endure, we allow ourselves to forget the death and destruction those very soldiers are responsible for" ("Trauma").

In sum, for Sacks, Lewis, and Scranton, much recent OEF/OIF writing—including, presumably, most of the works considered here—fails because its authors do not give readers the kind of wide-lens perspective necessary to wrestle with the troubling realities of the United States' recent wars. (The inclusion of the Qasim narrative in *War Porn* allows Scranton to steer around—if only narrowly—the pitfall he identifies in his essay.) Implicit in this critique is the assumption that these author-veterans have a responsibility to provide that perspective and lay bare those realities. My sense, however, is that a moral injury reading of these works gives the lie to this line of critique.

First off, I would contend that Sacks, Lewis, and Scranton go wrong in attributing the "restricted" perspective of contemporary war writing to unreflective patriotism, the popularity of embedding, or a blind fealty to common notions of trauma. Understanding the narrowness of perspective as related to moral injury—the signature wound of these wars—is simply a more accurate description of this formal trend. And to Scranton's critiques in particular, I would contend that the works considered here are not mindlessly reproducing trauma tropes; rather, they are intensively engaged in producing a truer, more helpful map of the mindscape of the modern service member.

Second, calling the pain of these works' protagonists moral injury—rather than trauma—automatically pushes "larger" questions of moral responsibility to the fore. Insofar as discussions of moral injury necessarily entail analysis of both micro-level moral breaches and macro-level moral responsibility, such discussions force *us* to tackle some of the challenges that Sacks, Lewis, and Scranton believe that the novelists in question here are evading. Klay gives us an instructive demonstration of that process in his story "Ten Kliks South." In it, a member of an artillery team is troubled as he thinks about the victims of the mortar rounds his team fires at targets miles away. At the outset, he wonders how responsibility for those deaths is apportioned among him and his fellow service members. But his question leads to others: if the whole firing team shares some of that responsibility, are there others who do too? "Why not the factory workers who made the ammo? . . . Or the taxpayers who paid for it?" (274). While some of his friends scoff at the questions, it is clear that the reader should not. And the structure of the piece requires that the reader move from observing one service member's moral pain to reflecting more broadly on civilian culpability for that pain.

We see this juxtaposition repeatedly in the works examined in this chapter, as our authors set the psychic suffering of service members up against the ignorance and evaded responsibility of home-front civilians. Deer notes that *The Yellow Birds* "represents a phase of the Iraq War when the occupation began to unravel catastrophically and the US home front's indifference to the war became clear" (320). We see that indifference when Bartle returns home to a largely apathetic American public; accordingly, Powers has Bartle quietly seethe as he thinks of the "spoiled cities of America" (215) that can ignore the pain of US troops and Iraqi civilians alike while "our little pest of a war rolled on" (216). Klay hits on this theme repeatedly throughout *Redeployment*. He is clearer in critiquing "spoiled" American civilians for their apathy and ignorance, seeing these qualities as indicative of more deeply entrenched moral failings: as the chaplain in "Prayer in the Furnace" says, "I have this sense that this place is holier than back home. Gluttonous, fat, oversexed, overconsuming, materialist home, where we're too lazy to see our own faults" (151). But for Klay, it seems as if American civilians are too lazy to see much of anything at all. The narrator of his first story is troubled by his neighbors' general ignorance—not only of the tactical details of the wars fought in their name but also of the very real dangers American troops are sent out to confront: "Outside, there're people walking around by the window like it's no big deal. People who have no idea where Fallujah is, where three members of your platoon died. People who've spent their whole lives at white" (12).

Of course, at some level, these "people" bear less responsibility than the politicians who send our children out to fight, and those politicians' growing indifference to the war in Iraq is even more galling: "It's all phony. . . . When the war started, almost three hundred congressmen voted for it. And seventy-seven senators. But now, everybody's washed their hands of it" (Klay 206). And yet Klay saves his most acerbic critiques for stateside liberals whose knee-jerk rejection of US war efforts serves as a coy mask for a more infuriating lack of reflection. We see this line of thinking most clearly in "Unless It's a Sucking Chest Wound," which has a Marine vet enrolling in an NYU graduate program after his return home. His interactions with his fellow students, many of whom arrive fresh from undergrad, reveal a troubling array of "knowing" attitudes toward the war:

> Few of them followed the wars at all, and most subscribed to a "It's a horrible mess, so let's not think about it too much" way of thinking. Then there were the political kids, who had definite opinions and were my least favorite to talk to. A lot of these overlapped with the insufferable public interest crowd, who hate the war . . . didn't

understand why anyone would ever join the military, didn't understand why anyone would ever want to own a gun, let alone fire one, but who still paid lip service to the idea that I deserved some sort of respect and that I was, in an imprecise way that was clearly related to action movies and recruiting commercials, far more "hard-core" than your average civilian. (250–51)

That Klay devotes so much time to such attitudes suggests that from his perspective, they might be more pernicious—or more recalcitrant—than "lazier" versions thereof. Scranton, it seems, would agree. His opening and closing chapters are set at a heavily caricatured 2004 barbecue hosted by a group of antiwar liberals. The music is Chopin, the hot debate question is whether or not anyone will move to Canada if Bush is reelected, and the menu is grilled tofu, vegan potato salad, and tabbouleh. The veteran Aaron is a late arrival, and Scranton puts the finishing touches on the satire when he has the freelance tech support guy Matt wonder aloud whether Aaron was "in the shit" (*War* 11). Matt, it seems, was not.

The question, of course, is how we might break through this miasma of unawareness—both self-righteous and otherwise. A poem by Turner called "Katyusha Rockets" offers a fantasy solution. Deer identifies Turner as one of the veteran-authors most devoted to piercing civilian ignorance about Iraq and Afghanistan. He writes, "Turner has sought to confront his readers with his (and their own) complicity with America's wars" (325). Turner's poem imagines what might happen if Americans couldn't remain spoiled and blind: a rocket fired in Iraq spans the ocean and comes down in Fresno, "the veteran's parade scattering at the impact, / mothers shielding their children by instinct, / old war vets crouching behind automobiles" (32). The message seems clear: civilians must come to know the realities of the wars fought in their name.

In all of these cases, not only does home-front apathy stand in stark relief against both the engagement and the suffering of US service members, but the apathy also might be understood as a driver of that engagement and suffering. To wit, these authors highlight civilian ignorance in order to suggest that it may well exacerbate the anguish of those who fight wars in our name. Service members' cognizance of that ignorance might spawn betrayal-based moral injury if they perceive civilians as fleeing their own responsibility for the war effort.

In closing, my hope is that attention to moral injury in these poems, stories, and novels shifts our focus from the putative responsibility of the authors writing OEF/OIF fiction to the responsibility of civilian readers. To imagine (as Sacks, Lewis, and Scranton do) that the great flaw of these authors—and veterans—is that they have not taken *enough* responsibility for the wars in Afghanistan and Iraq strikes me as wrongheaded. Rather, these works ask civilian readers to think about the ways in which they too might be complicit in the wrongs these authors describe, and to wonder whether they too should be morally injured by them.

Notes

1. Litz et al. see self-sacrifice as central to the moral code of the American soldier: "Dedicating oneself to live by a moral code and to protect the welfare of others requires a significant commitment to selflessness: to hold the welfare of others as inherently sacred and as potentially more important than one's own life and well-being" (*Adaptive* 39).

2. Brett Litz sees a similar mix of stressors in US involvement in Somalia; there, as in Afghanistan and Iraq, service members were troubled by "ambiguous, inconsistent or unacceptable rules of engagement (ROE); lack of clarity about the goals of the mission itself; a civilian population of combatants; and inherently contradictory experiences of the mission as both humanitarian and dangerous" (quoted in Wood, *What* 241). In remarks that David Wood sees as prescient, Litz wonders whether Somalia is "'the prototype of a new paradigm in military

operations,' one that 'may represent a unique class of potentially traumatizing experiences not sufficiently captured by traditional descriptors of war zone experience'" (242).

3. Such statements recall the Iraq veteran Matt Young's offhanded claim in his memoir *Eat the Apple* that "[e]veryone has PTSD" (238–39).

4. Eric Fair, the author of the Iraq torture memoir *Consequence*, makes similar statements. His suffering has nothing to do with the startle response—a signature symptom of PTSD. When town fireworks overshoot and land near him, he barely blinks (167).

5. Haytock argues that multivocal war novels are ethically preferable to books featuring a single narrative: "When deployed to tell war stories, multivoiced narration requires readers to consider the consequences of US military policy and to reassess whose life matters—whose life, in Judith Butler's terms, is 'grievable.' It also requires readers to reflect on the relationships among the characters and their stories; it insists that there are such relationships" (339).

6. Sacks suggests that the uniformity of contemporary war writing—and of this "first-person" perspective—is due to the fact that "[n]early all recent war writing has been cultivated in the hothouse of creative-writing programs. No wonder so much of it looks alike."

Coda

"WITNESSING" TO MORAL INJURY?

In wrapping up this volume, I turn to the seminal question of why we should pay attention to moral injury. It is certainly good to know that it exists, but should we devote attention to it? Does attending to it steal focus from the suffering of the traumatized? Or, to take a slightly different tack, does moral injury impose any responsibilities on bystanders? Might we think of ourselves as being ethically obliged to "witness" to MI?

The ethical turn in trauma theory happened long ago, and it is well established that certain traumas make moral demands of those who experience or learn about them. We speak of those demands in terms of testimony and witness. It is crucial that some trauma victims be given space to testify to the violence inflicted on them, especially if we hope to avoid such violence in the future. And it is equally crucial that others witness to their pain, either because encouraging them to tell the story of that pain might effect healing or because doing so might allow for justice and restitution. But do we have a similar responsibility to those who suffer the pain of moral injury? The answer here is not so straightforward. Some argue that the appropriate response to perpetration (and "perpetrator trauma") is simply condemnation. Dominick LaCapra claims that "moral norms" encourage "repulsion toward the perpetrator" (*Writing* 133). Certainly, such an approach seems appropriate in the case of history's most dastardly crimes, but it also might give way to a false sense of ethical purity and what Radstone calls a "Manicheanism" (25–26) that dictates that humans are either totally good or totally evil. As I have argued previously in this book, our approach to the morally injured must avoid such simplifications. For we would do well to remember, as Litz et al. remind us, that good people are capable of bad acts and bad people of good. Or perhaps we might go one step further in accepting that identifying *people* as good or bad is part of a bigger problem.

Yet we can say more. First, my sense is that Alan Gibbs is correct in suggesting that our attitude in addressing those suffering the pain of perpetration should not be "repulsion" but rather must begin with "analysis and understanding" (167)—and an acute sense of our own fallibility. (In an analogous situation, Primo Levi urges us to attend to those suffering the pain of perpetration with "pity and rigor, but that judgment of them be suspended" [60]). I add to these sensible claims a somewhat more provocative suggestion revealed in the previous chapters: that we *do* have a moral responsibility to witness to—and aid in the healing of—moral injury, at least in certain cases. This book has offered a number of specific situations in which moral injury witness might make sense. The novels and poems addressed in chapter 5 remind us that US civilians are at least partially responsible for MI among Afghanistan and Iraq War veterans, and that many of the actions that lead to their pain are both compulsory and carried out in the name of those back home. *The Fall* implies that the morally injured might be able to provide efficacious testimony for great historical traumas, if only we can help them heal. And chapter 3 reminds us that those with MI are capable of great good even

despite their misdeeds, and that those great goods will be possible
only if they can recuperate.

But can we offer any more general statements about MI witness?
In discussing the challenges involved in articulating an ethical response to moral injury, it is worthwhile to return to the exchange
between Cathy Caruth and Ruth Leys over the appropriate way of
addressing the pain of Tancred in *Gerusalemme Liberata*. Recall
that Leys rejects Caruth's identification of Tancred as a victim of
trauma after he mistakenly kills Clorinda. Here at greater length is
the final thrust of her critique:

> If, according to [Caruth's] analysis, the murderer Tancred can
> become the victim of the trauma and the voice of Clorinda
> testimony to *his* wound, then Caruth's logic would turn other
> perpetrators into victims too—for example, it would turn the
> executioners of the Jews into victims and the "cries" of the Jews
> into testimony to the trauma suffered by the Nazis. . . . On Ca-
> ruth's interpretation, what the parable of Tasso's story tells us is
> that not only can Tancred be considered the victim of trauma but
> that even the Nazis are not exempt from the same dispensation.
> (*Trauma* 297)

Leys's analysis is scathing, and there's no mistaking the vehemence
with which she objects to Caruth's approach. And yet we might ask,
what exactly is she objecting to? Certainly she refuses the notion
of Nazi victimhood, and in this she is not alone. Primo Levi does
the same in *The Drowned and the Saved*: "[T]o confuse [Nazis]
with their victims is a moral disease or an aesthetic affection or a
sinister sign of complicity; above all, it is precious service rendered
(intentionally or not) to the negators of truth" (48–49). But Leys
is not targeting only Nazis but any perpetrator who might be construed (or misconstrued) as a victim. Setting aside for a moment
the "category error" Michael Rothberg correctly identifies in such

claims (*Multidirectional* 90), we might wonder again why Leys opposes such a construal. The reason is simple but not unproblematic: perpetrators, it seems, are unworthy of witness. Theirs is a "suffering" that does not deserve "testimony." "Testimony" is a "dispensation," a grace from which perpetrators are exempted by their misdeeds. Here is a perfect example of a response to the pain of perpetration (MI) that is driven (in Gibbs's terms) not by "analysis and understanding" but by "repulsion." And while Leys's approach is understandable, it is also somewhat facile, and I think there are good reasons to argue that some if not most versions of moral injury might demand a brand of testimony analogous— and perhaps even identical—to trauma witness.

Some of these are unproblematic. Should we attend to the suffering of one who experiences without participating in great wrongs? Of course. Should we witness to the pain of the individual who is forced to breach his or her ethical code? Yes. (In the *Nicomachean Ethics*, Aristotle argues convincingly that one is not responsible for actions committed under compulsion.) But do we have a similar responsibility to witness to the pain of those who commit, enable, or are complicit in significant misdeeds? The answer comes to one's lips less quickly, but my sense is that that answer is still yes.

To make this case, we must first review why trauma witness is so important. (Agamben's distinction between the two Latin derivations of "witness" is germane here. I am concerned not with the "witness" who lives through and has direct experience of the traumatic event [*superstetes*], but with the responsibilities of third-party "witnesses" who have only mediated access to that event [*testis*] [17].) On a primary level, witnessing to an individual's trauma has therapeutic value. Dori Laub outlines this argument in one of the chapters in *Testimony*, claiming that attentively listening to stories of trauma might have both a liberating and a purgative power for those who suffer it. For Laub, trauma traps its victim, and therapeutic listening can help him or her decontaminate and escape:

> To undo this entrapment in a fate that cannot be known, cannot be told, but can only be repeated, a therapeutic process—a process of constructing a narrative, of reconstructing a history and essentially, of *re-externalizing the event*—has to be set in motion. This re-externalization of the event can occur and take effect only when one can articulate and *transmit* the story, literally transfer it to another outside oneself and then take it back again, inside. Telling thus entails a reassertion of the hegemony of reality and a re-externalization of the evil that affected and contaminated the trauma victim. (Felman and Laub 69)

Such a therapeutic approach to witness is presumably the one that Leys would rather we not apply to perpetrators; surely, we are not obliged to help liberate the Nazi from psychic pain.

Yet witnessing to trauma does not serve merely a therapeutic function. Laub indicates that witnessing may also allow for stories of atrocity to be told for the first time. He famously calls the Shoah an "event without a witness," in no small part because the Nazis hoped to eradicate all traces of their massive crime (Felman and Laub 80). Witnessing to the stories of survivors, then, undermines that effort and lets the details of that crime be revealed. (Such a responsibility would hold in all cases in which the unrepentant would rather great misdeed be buried; there are many.) Of course, we hope to reveal these details in order to keep such crimes from ever happening again. Or, to quote the Civil War photo caption Sontag cites in *Regarding the Pain of Others*, "Here are the dreadful details! Let them aid in preventing such another calamity from falling upon the nation" (53). But for Sontag, we witness to such details not only to keep particular histories from repeating themselves, but for the more general purpose of remembering. (It is

Agamben again who reminds us that the Greek word for witness is *martis*, which derives from the verb "to remember" [26].) Accordingly, she calls us not necessarily (or not only) to remember specific dark events but to think on what those events reveal about humanity's grisly potential: "Let the atrocious images haunt us," she writes. "Even if they are only tokens, and cannot possibly encompass most of the reality to which they refer, they still perform a vital function. The images say: This is what human beings are capable of doing—may volunteer to do, enthusiastically, self-righteously. Don't forget" (115).

So yes, we witness to trauma to help with healing. But we also witness to learn, to remember, to warn, and to prevent. And I contend that all of these latter responsibilities still hold in cases of moral injury. Indeed, instances of human cruelty on both the personal and the collective levels spawn both trauma and moral injury, and while we do not want to treat the two types of pain as ethical equivalents, we should nonetheless acknowledge that they may impose similar obligations on third parties.

I go one step further. If our goal is to staunch cruelty and calamity, we might sometimes be better off attending to them by witnessing to the pain of the morally injured. I say so in part because, as others have argued, trauma witness is often a more fraught process than perhaps we would like to admit. I note three pitfalls here. First, as Thomas Trezise points out, even when the well-intentioned listen to the stories of trauma victims, they sometimes fail to listen as well as they might, rushing past the most uncomfortable parts of the story. Trezise attributes such failures to a "desire to rescue survivors from their traumatic past" or a wish to "reduce tensions aroused in oneself by the witnessing of witnessing" (30).[1] Such failures go hand in hand with what LaCapra sees as a desire to airbrush trauma narratives, to make them neater, less tragic, or less disturbing. He argues that witnesses have a tendency to situate trauma in "fetishized and totalizing narratives that deny the trauma that called them into existence by prematurely (re) turning to the pleasure principle, harmonizing events, and often recuperating the past in terms of uplifting messages or optimistic, self-serving scenarios"—LaCapra views Spielberg's *Schindler's List* as a prime example of this "harmonizing" impulse at work (*Writing* 78). Of course, this urge comes from a good place; it derives from our sympathy for the traumatized and from a desire, we presume, to keep them from having to revisit their pain in its rawest form. And yet as Sontag contends, sympathy can be a counterproductive emotion when one tries to witness to unjust suffering. In such situations, sympathy tempts us to believe that there's little to be done about such pain and too quickly forecloses on the possibility that the witness might share some responsibility for it. "So far as we feel sympathy," she writes, "we feel we are not accomplices to what caused the suffering. Our sympathy proclaims our innocence as well as our impotence. To that extent, it can be (for all our good intentions) an impertinent—if not an inappropriate—response" (102–3).

To counteract these tendencies, and to avoid a facile sympathy for the victim, LaCapra urges the witness to develop and maintain a sense of "empathic unsettlement" when considering testimonies of both personal and collective trauma. Accordingly, we must let ourselves continue to be haunted by trauma and perhaps vulnerable to its sharp edges. Writes LaCapra,

> Empathic unsettlement poses a barrier to closure in discourse and places in jeopardy harmonizing or spiritually uplifting accounts of extreme events from which we attempt to derive reassurance or a benefit (for example, unearned confidence about the ability of the human spirit to endure any adversity with dignity and nobility).

The question is whether historiography in its own way may help not speciously to heal but to come to terms with the wounds and scars of the past. Such a coming-to-terms would seek knowledge whose truth claims are not one-dimensionally objectifying or narrowly cognitive but involve affect and may empathetically expose the self to unsettlement, if not a secondary trauma, which should not be glorified or fixated upon but addressed in a manner that strives to be cognitively and ethically responsible as well as open to the challenges of utopian aspiration. (*Writing* 40–41)

This last point is crucial: LaCapra is not arguing that we fetishize the trauma or seek out pain. But he does argue that our understanding of the causes of trauma (and our ability to fight against future iterations of them) will be unhelpfully simplistic if we do not work to recognize their continuing power to cut, hurt, and destroy.

But perhaps empathic unsettlement is difficult to maintain because its opposite (be it closure, comfort, or simple moving on) is so common. Time passes. We forgive. We heal. And even if we don't, we forget. So says Jean Améry: "Natural consciousness of time actually is rooted in the physiological process of wound-healing and became part of the social conception of reality" (quoted in Agamben 100). To hold on to wounds, then, is either unnatural or uncommon. And yet for Améry, a resistance fighter and camp survivor himself, we have a moral responsibility to allow some wounds to stay fresh. He argues that in certain cases, notably his own, there is ethical value not in forgiveness but in resentment. "A forgiving and forgetting induced by social pressure is immoral," he writes, adding,

My resentments are there in order that the crime become a moral reality for the criminal, in order that he be swept into the truth of his atrocity. . . . What happened, happened. This sentence is just as

> true as it is hostile to morals and intellect. . . . The moral person de-
> mands annulment of time—in the particular case under question,
> by nailing the criminal to his deed. (quoted in Agamben 100)

For Améry, resentment has a positive ethical value because it helps him maintain a healthy sense of hostility toward atrocity and keeps him (and us) meditating on issues of responsibility and prevention while avoiding pat or unearned moves toward closure and comfort. Or, put more forcefully, resentment is a more effective driver of the empathic unsettlement that keeps us in touch with (and disturbed by) the crimes that often produce both trauma and moral injury. Hence, in certain circumstances, if what Améry says is true, resentment can be a firmer foundation on which to build effective witness.

Hence, my argument here is that at least in some cases, moral injury witness is an effective approach to atrocity and cruelty insofar as it is more likely to inspire resentment and the empathic unsettlement that LaCapra says is crucial for maintaining witness. Let me provide just one example. When prisoners arrived at Auschwitz, their possessions were collected by another group of inmates often referred to as the "Kanada Kommando"—or simply Canada. Members of the Kanada Kommando were responsible for sorting the possessions and arranging for the shipment of valuables back to the Reich. However, assignment to Canada was understood as a small privilege in the camps, as members slept in barracks and, if they were careful, could steal food and other necessaries from the piles of goods they handled. Of course, this is ghastly work—and a prime example of the ways in which the Nazis further degraded inmates by making them complicit in the horrors of the camps. Levi calls this and similar transfers of responsibility the Nazis' "most demonic crime." Writing of the Sonderkommando—which were constructed with a similar logic in mind—he notes, "Behind the pragmatic aspect (to economize on able men, to impose on others the most atrocious tasks) other more subtle aspects can be perceived. This institution represented an attempt to shift onto others—specifically, the victims—the burden of guilt, so that they were deprived of even the solace of innocence" (53). Witnessing to such atrocities is remarkably difficult, Levi writes: "It is neither easy nor agreeable to dredge this abyss of viciousness, and yet I think it must be done, because what could be perpetrated yesterday could be attempted again tomorrow, could overwhelm us and our children" (53). How best, then, to dredge?

Dori Laub articulates a trauma witness approach to Canada in *Testimony*. In the process of interviewing one of the contributors to Yale's Fortunoff Video Archive for Holocaust Testimonies, he realizes from details in her narrative that she was likely a member of the Kommando: "She emphasized with pride the way in which, upon returning, she would supply [clothes and shoes] to her fellow inmates, thus saving the lives of some of them who literally had no shoes to walk in and no clothes to protect them from the frost" (Felman and Laub 60). Laub asks her, then, whether she was part of Canada; startled, she says no, at which point Laub stops the line of questioning. Why does he stop? It seems obvious: he quits out of sympathy and tact. In his words, he does not press further out of a sense of "respect" and from a desire "not to upset, not to trespass" (60–61). His decision is thoroughly understandable—even laudable—but even he admits that it keeps him from asking a number of valuable follow-up questions: "We did not talk of the sorting out of the belongings of the dead. She did not think of them as the remainings of the thousands who were gassed. She did not ask herself where they had come from. The presents she brought back to her fellow inmates, the better, newer clothes and shoes, had for her no origin" (60). Trezise argues that Laub might have justifiably continued—and that pressing the woman on the details of her testimony might be construed as a "welcoming" move: "[H]olding the witness accountable to certain objective standards in order to fulfill the responsibility of listening for others might well be considered a way of welcoming the witness herself into the community of these listeners" (25). Perhaps. At the very least, it is worth noting that Laub, in seeking to avoid upsetting and trespassing, is not cultivating the empathic unsettlement that LaCapra says is necessary to the most valuable forms of witness. And he is not, to use Levi's word once more, "dredging."

It is worth noting here that nothing in the woman's testimony suggests that she is morally injured by her experience in Canada. She looks back on her decisions with "pride." For contrast, then, we might turn to Borowski's oft-anthologized short story "This Way for the Gas, Ladies and Gentlemen." The Auschwitz survivor's story focuses on a group of men in the Kanada Kommando and centers on the experience of the narrator, who is generally read as a stand-in for Borowski himself. The characters in the story cope in different ways. A giant Ukrainian named Andrei alternates between brutal violence and stoic silence while self-medicating with vodka. A Frenchman, Henri, retreats to a faux-philosophical distance: "Ah, on the contrary, it is natural, predictable, calculated. . . . Why, I'd even call it healthy. It's simple logic, *compris*?" (2257). The narrator of the piece, however, breaks down: "I look up, but the face swims before my eyes, dissolves, huge and transparent, melts into the motionless trees and the sea of people. . . . I blink rapidly: Henri. 'Listen, Henri, are we good people?'" (2257). The speaker fears that he is being degraded by the work; he worries that his compelled participation in the machinery of genocide has begun to damage his sense of himself as a moral being.

This, of course, is the voice of moral injury, and "This Way for the Gas" can be productively read as an MI narrative. It is also worth noting that it provides the deep dive that Levi believes is necessary if we are to witness to the most horrific crimes. Borowski answers all the questions that Laub avoids in his interview with another member of the Kommando—about the "sorting out of the belongings of the dead," the "remainings of the . . . gassed," the origin of the "newer clothes and shoes"—and many others Laub doesn't dare pursue. Unsurprisingly, then, "This Way for the Gas" is a deeply disturbing story, because of both the answers it provides and the ways it forces us to wrestle with the narrator's complicity. Do we "resent" the speaker for his actions? No. But does his narrative stoke empathic unsettlement? Absolutely. There is no closure here. No forgiveness. Only detailed meditation on demonic crime. Further, Borowski's story demands our attention—and our witness. And it demonstrates the potential value of witnessing to and through moral injury narratives.

Of course, I would be remiss if I didn't point out the crucial distinction between the trauma testimony of Laub's interlocutor and Borowski's tale, colored by MI themes: the first is autobiography while the second, even if it is colored by the author's experience, is fiction. Therefore, I close this book with a few words on the testimonial value of literature that engages moral injury themes.

Bryan Doerries is the artistic director of Theater of War Productions, a troupe that presents readings of classical Greek plays (primarily Sophocles's *Ajax* and *Philoctetes*) to military and civilian audiences in the United States and Europe. In his 2015 book *The Theater of War*, he argues that ancient tragedies—especially in performance—can help illuminate "the moral and spiritual dimensions of trauma" (8). And yet Doerries isn't particularly interested in what these plays can teach us, or in what they say;

he's more interested in what they *do*. For the director hopes that these productions do not merely educate, but that they can heal. In his book, he tells a story about one of these readings, staged for a group of service members in Germany. After the production ended, Doerries opened a Q and A with a simple question that he often asks in such settings: "Why do you think Sophocles wrote this play?" One service member raised his hand and said, "He wrote it to boost morale." Pressed as to how this tragedy about a soldier's depression, violence, and suicide might boost morale, the young man continued: "It's the truth . . . and we're all here watching it together" (4). Doerries and everyone else who runs the theater believe that seeing "the truth" of the psychological problems that service members suffer can help veterans cope with them. As the troupe's website (and effective mission statement) reads, plays like *Ajax*

> timelessly and universally depict the visible and invisible wounds of war. By presenting these plays to military and civilian audiences, our hope is to de-stigmatize psychological injury, increase awareness of post-deployment psychological health issues, disseminate information regarding available resources, and foster greater family, community, and troop resilience. Using Sophocles' plays to forge a common vocabulary for openly discussing the impact of war on individuals, families, and communities, these events will be aimed at generating compassion and understanding between diverse audiences. ("About Us")

This paragraph might as well be an epigraph for this book as well, for I share Doerries's hope that creative literature—not just plays but novels, stories, and poems—has the power to get us closer to "the truth" of our invisible wounds, among them moral injury. And I contend that merely disseminating such information may have healing power, especially in a moment when MI is hurting multitudes but is known by few. In a *New York Times Magazine* cover story on MI from June 2018, Eyal Press quotes the military psychologist Wayne Chappelle as saying that MI is still "not widely accepted by the military or the psychological community." That so many of our service members and veterans might suffer from a condition that is neither widely understood nor accepted suggests that any efforts to raise awareness about it, whether in the world or in literature, are worthwhile.

Note

1. Trezise sees an example of this habit in Dori Laub's willingness to gloss over certain factual inconsistencies in the account of a camp survivor who was present at the Auschwitz prisoners' revolt (23–25).

Works Cited

"About Us." Theater of War Productions. n.d. Web. 14 August 2018.

Aeschylus. *The Oresteia*. Trans. Robert Fagles. New York: Penguin, 1979.

Agamben, Giorgio. *Remnants of Auschwitz: The Witness and the Archive*. Trans. Daniel Heller-Roazen. New York: Zone Books, 1999.

Alexander, Jeffrey, et al. *Cultural Trauma and Collective Identity*. Berkeley: University of California Press, 2004.

Allan, Derek. "The Power of an Idea: Raskolnikov in *Crime and Punishment*." *Literary Imagination* 18.2 (2016): 133–48.

Audergon, Arlene. "Collective Trauma: The Nightmare of History." *Psychotherapy and Politics International* 2.1 (2004): 16–31.

Bakhtin, Mikhail. *Problems of Dostoevsky's Poetics*. Ed. and trans. Caryl Emerson. Minneapolis: University of Minnesota Press, 1984.

Bataille, Georges. *The Accursed Share: An Essay on General Economy*. Trans. Robert Hurley. Vol. 1. 1967. New York: Zone Books, 1991.

——. *Literature and Evil*. Trans. Alastair Hamilton. 1957. London: Marion Boyars, 1990.

Belknap, Robert L. "Dostoevskii and Psychology." *The Cambridge Companion to Dostoevskii*. Ed. W. J. Leatherbarrow. Cambridge: Cambridge University Press, 2002. 131–47.

Bernstein, J. M. *Torture and Dignity: An Essay on Moral Injury*. Chicago: University of Chicago Press, 2015.

Blake, Elizabeth. "Sonya, Silent No More: A Response to the Woman Question in Dostoevsky's *Crime and Punishment*." *Slavic and East European Journal* 50.2 (2006): 252–71.

Borowski, Tadeusz. "This Way for the Gas, Ladies and Gentlemen." *The Norton Anthology of Western Literature*. Ed. Martin Puchner. Vol. 2. New York: Norton, 2014. 2248–62.

Brancu, Mira, et al. "The Post-deployment Mental Health (PDMH) Study and Repository: A Multi-site Study of US Afghanistan and Iraq Era Veterans." *International Journal of Methods in Psychiatric Research* 26.3 (2017): 1–22.

Breger, Louis. *Dostoevsky: The Author as Psychoanalyst.* New York: New York University Press, 1989.

Brock, Rita Nakashima, and Gabriella Lettini. *Exploring Moral Injury in Sacred Texts.* Philadelphia: Jessica Kingsley, 2017.

——. *Soul Repair: Recovering from Moral Injury after War.* Boston: Beacon, 2013.

Brooks, David. "The Moral Injury." *New York Times.* 17 February 2015. Web.

Bruckner, Pascal. *The Tyranny of Guilt: An Essay on Western Masochism.* Princeton, NJ: Princeton University Press, 2010.

Bryan, Craig J., et al. "Moral Injury, Posttraumatic Stress Disorder, and Suicidal Behavior among National Guard Personnel." *Psychological Trauma: Theory, Research, Practice, and Policy* 10.1 (2018): 36–45.

Bryce, Robert. "I Am Sullied—No More." *Texas Observer.* 9 March 2007. Web.

Camus, Albert. *Camus at Combat: Writing, 1944–1947.* Trans. Arthur Goldhammer. Princeton, NJ: Princeton University Press, 2007.

——. *The Fall.* Trans. Justin O'Brien. 1957. New York: Vintage International, 1984.

Caruth, Cathy. "An Interview with Geoffrey Hartman." *Studies in Romanticism* 35.4 (1996): 630–52.

——., ed. *Trauma: Explorations in Memory.* Baltimore: Johns Hopkins University Press, 1995.

——. *Unclaimed Experience.* Baltimore: Johns Hopkins University Press, 1996.

Coleridge, Samuel Taylor. "Rime of the Ancient Mariner." *Select Poems.* Ed. Andrew J. George. Boston: D. C. Heath, 1902. 109–38.

Corrigan, Yuri. "Dostoevskii on Evil as Safe Haven and Anesthetic." *Slavic and East European Journal* 63.2 (2019): 226–43.

Cowell, Alan. "Oscar Pistorius at Increasing Risk of Suicide, Lawyer Says." *New York Times.* 2 July 2014. Web.

Craps, Stef. *Postcolonial Witnessing: Trauma Out of Bounds.* New York: Palgrave Macmillan, 2013.

Crisford, Hannah, et al. "Offence-Related Posttraumatic Stress Disorder (PTSD) Symptomatology and Guilt in Mentally Disordered Violent and Sexual Offenders." *Journal of Forensic Psychiatry and Psychology* 19.1 (2008): 86–107.

Crownshaw, Rick. "Rereading Der Vorleser, Remembering the Perpetrator." *Germans as Victims in the Literary Fiction of the Berlin Republic*. Ed. Stuart Taberner and Karina Berger. Woodbridge, UK: Boydell and Brewer, 2009. 147–61.

Currier, Joseph M., et al. "Development and Evaluation of the Expressions of Moral Injury Scale—Military Version." *Clinical Psychology and Psychotherapy* 25 (2018): 474–88.

Currier, Joseph M., et al. "Initial Psychometric Evaluation of the Moral Injury Questionnaire—Military Version." *Clinical Psychology and Psychotherapy* 22 (2015): 54–63.

Curtler, Hugh Mercer. "The Artistic Failure of *Crime and Punishment*." *Journal of Aesthetic Education* 38.1 (2004): 1–11.

Danieli, Yael. "Introduction: History and Conceptual Foundations." *International Handbook of Multigenerational Legacies of Trauma*. Ed. Yael Danieli. New York: Plenum, 1998. 1–20.

Davis, Colin. "What Happened?: Camus's *La Chute*, Shoshana Felman and the Witnessing of Trauma." *French Forum* 36.1 (2011): 37–53.

De Jong, Joop, and Ria Reis. "Collective Trauma Processing: Dissociation as a Way of Processing Postwar Traumatic Stress." *Transcultural Psychiatry* 50.5 (2013): 644–61.

Deer, Patrick. "Beyond Recovery: Representing History and Memory in Iraq War Writing." *Modern Fiction Studies* 63.2 (2017): 312–35.

DeRosa, Aaron, and Stacey Peebles. "Enduring Operations: Narratives of the Contemporary Wars." *Modern Fiction Studies* 63.2 (2017): 203–24.

Di Prete, Laura. "Don DeLillo's *The Body Artist*: Performing the Body, Narrating Trauma." *Contemporary Literature* 46.3 (2005): 483–510.

Doerries, Bryan. *The Theater of War: What Ancient Greek Tragedies Can Teach Us Today*. New York: Alfred A. Knopf, 2015.

Dostoevsky, Fyodor. *Crime and Punishment*. Trans. Richard Pevear and Larissa Volokhonsky. New York: Alfred A. Knopf, 1993.

Drescher, Kent D., et al. "An Exploration of the Viability and Usefulness of the Construct of Moral Injury in War Veterans." *Traumatology* 17.1 (2011): 8–13.

Eliot, George. *Adam Bede*. 1859. New York: Doubleday, 1901.

Erikson, Kai. *A New Species of Trouble: Explorations in Disaster, Trauma, and Community*. New York: Norton, 1994.

——. "Notes on Trauma and Community." *American Imago* 48.4 (1991): 455–72.

——. "Trauma at Buffalo Creek." *Society* 35.2 (1998): 153–61.

Fair, Eric. *Consequence: A Memoir*. New York: Holt, 2016.

Farnsworth, Jacob K., et al. "A Functional Approach to Understanding and Treating Military-Related Moral Injury." *Journal of Contextual Behavioral Science* 6 (2017): 391–97.

Farnsworth, Jacob K., et al. "The Role of Moral Emotions in Military Trauma: Implications for the Study and Treatment of Moral Injury." *Review of General Psychology* 18.4 (2014): 249–62.

Felman, Shoshana, and Dori Laub. *Testimony: Crises of Witnessing in Literature, Psychoanalysis, and History*. New York: Routledge, 1992.

Ferdowsi, Abolqasem. *Shahnameh*. Trans. Dick Davis. New York: Penguin, 2016.

Finkel, David. *Thank You for Your Service*. New York: Farrar, Straus and Giroux, 2013.

Flipse Vargas, Alison, et al. "Moral Injury Themes in Combat Veterans' Narrative Responses from the National Vietnam Veterans' Readjustment Study." *Traumatology* 19.3 (2013): 243–50.

Frank, Joseph. *Dostoevsky: The Miraculous Years, 1865–1871*. Princeton, NJ: Princeton University Press, 1995.

Frank, Joseph, and David I. Goldstein. *Selected Letters of Fyodor Dostoyevsky*. Trans. Andrew R. MacAndrew. New Brunswick, NJ: Rutgers University Press, 1987.

Frankfurt, Sheila B., et al. "Indirect Relations between Transgressive Acts and General Combat Exposure and Moral Injury." *Military Medicine* 182.11/12 (2017): 1950–56.

Frankfurt, Sheila, and Patricia Frazier. "A Review of Research on Moral Injury in Combat Veterans." *Military Psychology* 28.5 (2016): 318–30.

Gibbs, Alan. *Contemporary American Trauma Narratives*. Edinburgh: Edinburgh University Press, 2014.

Gray, Matt J., et al. "When Self-Blame Is Rational and Appropriate: The Limited Utility of Socratic Questioning in the Context of Moral Injury: Commentary on Wachen et al. (2016)." *Cognitive and Behavioral Practice* 24 (2017): 383–87.

Grossman, Dave. *On Killing: The Psychological Cost of Learning to Kill in War and Society*. New York: Back Bay Books, 2009.

Haight, Wendy, et al. "Everyday Coping with Moral Injury: The Perspectives of Professionals and Parents Involved with Child Protection Services." *Children and Youth Services Review* 82 (2017): 108–21.

Hartman, Geoffrey. "On Traumatic Knowledge and Literary Studies." *New Literary History* 26.3 (1995): 537–63.

Haytock, Jennifer. "Reframing War Stories: Multivoiced Novels of the Wars in Iraq and Afghanistan." *Modern Fiction Studies* 63.2 (2017): 336–54.

Held, Philip, et al. "Using Prolonged Exposure and Cognitive Processing Therapy to Treat Veterans with Moral Injury-Based PTSD: Two Case Examples." *Cognitive and Behavioral Practice* 25.3 (2018): 377–90.

Helmling, Stephen. "Failure and the Sublime: Fredric Jameson's Writing in the '80s." *Postmodern Culture* 10.3 (2000): 6.

Hénaff, Marcel. *Sade: The Invention of the Libertine Body*. Minneapolis: University of Minnesota Press, 1999.

Herman, Judith. *Trauma and Recovery*. New York: Basic Books, 1992.

Hesford, Wendy S. "Reading Rape Stories: Material Rhetoric and the Trauma of Representation." *College English* 62.2 (1999): 192–221.

Iraq Veterans against the War, and Aaron Glantz. *Winter Soldier, Iraq and Afghanistan: Eyewitness Accounts of the Occupations*. Chicago: Haymarket Books, 2008.

Jameson, Fredric. "Pleasure: A Political Issue." In *The Syntax of History*, 61–74. Vol. 2 of *The Ideologies of Theory: Essays 1971–1986*. Minneapolis: University of Minnesota Press, 1988.

——. "Postmodernism; or, The Cultural Logic of Late Capitalism." *Postmodernism and Popular Culture: A Cultural History*. Ed. John Docker. Cambridge: Cambridge University Press, 1994. 53–92.

——. *The Syntax of History*. Minneapolis: University of Minnesota Press, 1988.

Jinkerson, Jeremy D. "Defining and Assessing Moral Injury: A Syndrome Perspective." *Traumatology* 22.2 (2016): 122–30.

Johnson, Christopher D. *Hyperboles: The Rhetoric of Excess in Baroque Literature and Thought*. Cambridge, MA: Harvard University Press, 2010.

Just, Daniel. "From Guilt to Shame: Albert Camus and Literature's Ethical Response to Politics." *MLN* 125.4 (2010): 895–912.

Kantsteiner, Wulf. "Genealogy of a Category Mistake: A Critical Intellectual History of the Cultural Trauma Metaphor." *Rethinking History* 8.2 (2004): 193–221.

Karenian, Hatsantour, et al. "Collective Trauma Transmission and Traumatic Reactions among Descendants of Armenian Refugees." *International Journal of Social Psychiatry* 57.4 (2010): 327–37.

Katchadourian, Herant. *Guilt: The Bite of Conscience*. Stanford, CA: Stanford University Press, 2010.

Kidd, James. "American Soldier-Poet Brian Turner Reveals the Enduring Turmoil That Inspired His Memoir." *Independent*. 30 August 2014. Web.

Klay, Phil. *Redeployment*. New York: Penguin, 2014.

Koenig, Harold G., et al. "Rationale for Spiritually Oriented Cognitive Processing Therapy for Moral Injury in Active Duty Military and Veterans with Posttraumatic Stress Disorder." *Journal of Nervous and Mental Disease* 205.2 (2017): 147–53.

Kopacz, Marek S., et al. "Moral Injury: A New Challenge for Complementary and Alternative Medicine." *Complementary Therapies in Medicine* 24 (2016): 29–33.

LaCapra, Dominick. *History and Memory after Auschwitz.* Ithaca, NY: Cornell University Press, 1998.

———. *Representing the Holocaust: History, Theory, Trauma.* Ithaca, NY: Cornell University Press, 1994.

———. "Revisiting the Historians' Debate: Mourning and Genocide." *History and Memory* 9.1/2 (1997): 80–112.

———. *Writing History, Writing Trauma.* 2001. Baltimore: Johns Hopkins University Press, 2014.

Levi, Primo. *The Drowned and the Saved.* Trans. Raymond Rosenthal. New York: Summit Books, 1986.

Leys, Ruth. *From Guilt to Shame: Auschwitz and After.* Princeton, NJ: Princeton University Press, 2007.

———. *Trauma: A Genealogy.* Chicago: University of Chicago Press, 2000.

Litz, Brett, et al. *Adaptive Disclosure: A New Treatment for Military Trauma, Loss, and Moral Injury.* New York: Guilford, 2016.

Litz, Brett, et al. "Moral Injury and Moral Repair in War Veterans: A Preliminary Model and Intervention Strategy." *Clinical Psychology Review* 29 (2009): 695–706.

Litz, Brett T., and Patricia K. Kerig. "Introduction to the Special Issue on Moral Injury: Conceptual Challenges, Methodological Issues, and Clinical Applications." *Journal of Traumatic Stress* 32 (2019): 341–49.

Luckhurst, Roger. "In War Times: Fictionalizing Iraq." *Contemporary Literature* 53.4 (2012): 713–37.

———. "Iraq War Body Counts: Reportage, Photography, and Fiction." *Modern Fiction Studies* 63.2 (2017): 355–72.

———. *The Trauma Question.* New York: Routledge, 2008.

Luhrmann, T. M. "The Traumatized Social Self: The Parsi Predicament in in Modern Bombay." *Cultures under Siege: Collective Violence and Trauma.* Ed. Antonius C. G. M. Robben and Marcelo M. Suárez-Orozco. Cambridge: Cambridge University Press, 2000. 158–93.

Lyall, Sarah. "After Sobs, Prayers and Illness in Court, Pistorius May Testify." *New York Times.* 2 April 2014. Web.

MacNair, Rachel M. *Perpetration-Induced Traumatic Stress: The Psychological Consequences of Killing.* Westport, CT: Praeger, 2002.

Maguen, Shira, et al. "The Impact of Killing in War on Mental Health Symptoms and Related Functioning." *Journal of Traumatic Stress* 22 (2009): 435–43.

Maguen, Shira, and Brett Litz. "Moral Injury in Veterans of War." *PTSD Research Quarterly* 23 (2012): 1–6.

Marshall, S. L. A. *Men against Fire: The Problem of Battle Command.* 1947. Norman: University of Oklahoma Press, 2000.

McAvan, Em. "Paranoia in Spook Country: William Gibson and the Technological Sublime of the War on Terror." *Journal of Postcolonial Writing* 46.3/4 (2010): 405–13.

McCormack, Lynne, and Lisa Riley. "Medical Discharge from the 'Family,' Moral Injury, and a Diagnosis of PTSD: Is Psychological Growth Possible in the Aftermath of Policing Trauma?" *Traumatology* 22.1 (2016): 19–28.

McGlothlin, Erin. "Theorizing the Perpetrator in Bernhard Schlink's *The Reader* and Martin Amis's *Time's Arrow.*" *After Representation?* Ed. R. Clifton Spargo and Robert M. Ehrenreich. New Brunswick, NJ: Rutgers University Press, 2010. 210–30.

McNally, Richard J. *Remembering Trauma.* Cambridge, MA: Harvard University Press, 2003.

Miller, T. Christian. "A Journey That Ended in Anguish." *Los Angeles Times.* 27 November 2005. Web.

Mochulsky, Konstantin. *Dostoevsky: His Life and Work.* Trans. Michael A Minihan. Princeton, NJ: Princeton University Press, 1967.

Mohamed, Saira. "Of Monsters and Men: Perpetrator Trauma and Mass Atrocity." *Columbia Law Review* 115.5 (2015): 1157–216.

Morag, Raya. *Waltzing with Bashir: Perpetrator Trauma and Cinema.* London: I. B. Tauris, 2013.

Morris, David J. *The Evil Hours: A Biography of Post-traumatic Stress Disorder.* New York: Houghton Mifflin Harcourt, 2015.

Morrison, Toni. *Beloved.* 1987. New York: Plume, 1988.

Murray, E., et al. "Are Medical Students in Prehospital Care at Risk of Moral Injury?" *Emergency Medicine Journal* 35.8 (2018): 590–94. Web.

Nash, William P., et al. "Psychometric Evaluation of the Moral Injury Events Scale." *Military Medicine* 178 (2013): 646–52.

Nash, William P., and Brett T. Litz. "Moral Injury: A Mechanism for War-Related Psychological Trauma in Military Family Members." *Clinical Child Family Psychology Review* 16 (2013): 365–75.

Nelson, Cary. "Teaching and Editing at World's End: Collective Trauma and Individual Witness in American Holocaust Poetry." *American Studies* 57.2 (2012): 221–44.

Novak, Amy. "Who Speaks? Who Listens?: The Problem of Address in Two Nigerian Trauma Novels." *Studies in the Novel* 40.1/2 (2008): 31–51.

Nunokawa, Jeff. "Eros and Isolation: The Antisocial George Eliot." *ELH* 69.4 (2002): 835–60.

O'Brien, Tim. *In the Lake of the Woods.* 1994. New York: Penguin, 1995.

Onishi, Norimitsu. "Oscar Pistorius Sentenced to 6 Years in Reeva Steenkamp Murder." *New York Times.* 6 July 2016. Web.

Packer, George. "Home Fires." *New Yorker.* 7 April 2014. Web.

Papanastassiou, Maria, et al. "Post-traumatic Stress Disorder in Mentally Ill Perpetrators of Homicide." *Journal of Forensic Psychiatry and Psychology* 15.1 (2004): 66–75.

Pederson, Joshua. "Moral Injury in Literature." *Narrative* 28.1 (2020): 43–61.

——. "Speak, Trauma: Toward a Revised Understanding of Literary Trauma Theory." *Narrative* 22.3 (2014): 333–53.

Peebles, Stacey. *Welcome to the Suck: Narrating the American Soldier's Experience in Iraq.* Ithaca, NY: Cornell University Press, 2011.

Powers, Brian S. "Moral Injury and Original Sin: The Applicability of Augustinian Moral Psychology in Light of Combat Trauma." *Theology Today* 73.4 (2017): 325–37.

Powers, Kevin. *The Yellow Birds.* New York: Back Bay Books, 2012.

Press, Eyal. "The Wounds of the Drone Warrior." *New York Times Magazine.* 13 June 2018. Web.

Puniewska, Maggie. "A Soldier's Guilt: Healing a Wounded Sense of Morality." *Atlantic.* 3 July 2015. Web. 12 January 2016.

Radstone, Susannah. "Trauma Theory: Contexts, Politics, Ethics." *Paragraph* 30.1 (2007): 9–29.

Rice, James L. *Dostoevsky and the Healing Art: An Essay in Literary and Medical History.* Ann Arbor, MI: Ardis, 1985.

Robben, Antonius C. G. M. "The Assault on Basic Trust: Disappearance, Protest, and Reburial in Argentina." *Cultures under Siege: Collective Violence and Trauma.* Ed. Antonius C. G. M. Robben and Marcelo M. Suárez-Orozco. Cambridge: Cambridge University Press, 2000. 70–101.

Rogers, Paul, et al. "Behavioral Treatment of PTSD in a Perpetrator of Manslaughter: A Single Case Study." *Journal of Traumatic Stress* 13.3 (2000): 511–19.

Ronner, Amy D. "Dostoevsky and the Therapeutic Jurisprudence Confession." *John Marshall Law Review* 41 (2006): 41–113.

Rothberg, Michael. "Beyond Tancred and Clorinda: Trauma Studies for Implicated Subjects." *The Future of Trauma Theory: Contemporary Literary and Cultural Criticism.* Ed. Gert Buelens, Sam Durrant, and Robert Eaglestone. New York: Routledge, 2014. xi–xviii.

———. *The Implicated Subject: Beyond Victims and Perpetrators*. Stanford, CA: Stanford University Press, 2019.

———. *Multidirectional Memory: Remembering the Holocaust in the Age of Decolonization*. Stanford, CA: Stanford University Press, 2009.

Sacks, Sam. "First-Person Shooters: What's Missing in Contemporary War Fiction." *Harper's Magazine*. August 2015. Web.

Sanyal, Debarati. *Memory and Complicity: Migrations of Holocaust Remembrance*. New York: Fordham University Press, 2015.

———. "Torture, Allegory, and Memory in Sartre." *Yale French Studies* 118/119 (2010): 52–71.

Sartre, Jean-Paul. *The Condemned of Altona*. Trans. Sylvia and George Leeson. New York: Vintage Books, 1963.

Saul, Jack. *Collective Trauma, Collective Healing: Promoting Community Resilience in the Aftermath of Disaster*. Florence, UK: Routledge, 2013.

Schmidle, Nicholas. "In the Crosshairs." *New Yorker*. 3 June 2013. Web.

Scranton, Roy. "The Trauma Hero: From Wilfred Owen to *Redeployment* and *American Sniper*." *Los Angeles Review of Books*. 25 January 2015. Web.

———. *War Porn*. New York: Soho, 2016.

Shakespeare, William. *King Lear*. Ed. David Nichol Smith. Boston: D. C. Heath, 1917.

———. *Macbeth*. Ed. F. A. Purcell and L. M. Somers. Chicago: Scott, Foresman, 1916.

Shay, Jonathan. *Achilles in Vietnam: Combat Trauma and the Undoing of Character*. 1994. New York: Scribner, 2003.

———. "Moral Injury." *Intertexts* 16.1 (2012): 57–66.

———. *Odysseus in America: Combat Trauma and the Trials of Homecoming*. 2002. New York: Scribner, 2010.

Sherman, Nancy. *Afterwar: Healing the Moral Wounds of Our Soldiers*. Oxford: Oxford University Press, 2015.

Sicher, Efraim. "'Tancred's Wound': From Repression to Symbolization of the Holocaust in Second-Generation Narratives." *Journal of Modern Jewish Studies* 5.2 (2006): 189–201.

Silko, Leslie Marmon. *Ceremony*. 1977. New York: Penguin, 1986.

Sindicich, Natasha, et al. "Offenders as Victims: Post-traumatic Stress Disorder and Substance Use Disorder among Male Prisoners." *Journal of Forensic Psychiatry and Psychology* 25.1 (2014): 44–60.

Sontag, Susan. *Regarding the Pain of Others*. New York: Picador, 2003.

Suárez-Orozco, Marcelo M., and Antonius C. G. M. Robben. "Interdisciplinary Perspectives on Violence and Trauma." *Cultures under Siege: Collective*

Violence and Trauma. Ed. Antonius C. G. M. Robben and Marcelo M. Suárez-Orozco. Cambridge: Cambridge University Press, 2000. 1–42.

Suleiman, Susan Rubin. "When the Perpetrator Becomes a Reliable Witness of the Holocaust: On Jonathan Littell's *Les Bienveillantes.*" *New German Critique* 36.1 (2009): 1–19.

Sütterlin, Nicole. *Poetics of the Wound: The Discovery of Trauma in Nineteenth-Century Literature.* Göttingen: Wallstein, forthcoming.

Taberner, Stuart. *German Literature of the 1990s and Beyond.* Woodbridge, UK: Boydell and Brewer, 2005.

Taberner, Stuart, and Karina Berger, eds. *Germans as Victims in the Literary Fiction of the Berlin Republic.* Rochester, NY: Camden House, 2009.

Tasso, Torquato. *Jerusalem Delivered.* Trans. Anthony M. Esolen. Baltimore: Johns Hopkins University Press, 2000.

Tick, Edward. *Warrior's Return: Restoring the Soul after War.* Boulder, CO: Sounds True, 2014.

Todd, Olivier. *Albert Camus: A Life.* Trans. Benjamin Ivry. New York: Alfred A. Knopf, 1997.

Trezise, Thomas. *Witnessing Witnessing: On the Reception of Holocaust Survivor Testimony.* New York: Fordham University Press, 2013.

Tucker, Janet G. *Profane Challenge and Orthodox Response in Dostoevsky's "Crime and Punishment."* Amsterdam: Rodopi, 2008.

Turner, Brian. *Here, Bullet.* Farmington, ME: Alice James Books, 2005.

Vertzberger, Yaacov Y. I. "The Antinomies of Collective Political Trauma: A Pre-Theory." *Political Psychology* 18.4 (1997): 863–76.

Vice, Sue. "Exploring the Fictions of Perpetrator Suffering." *Journal of Literature and Trauma Studies* 2.1/2 (2013): 15–25.

Visser, Irene. "Trauma Theory and Postcolonial Literary Studies." *Journal of Postcolonial Writing* 47.3 (2011): 270–82.

Wachen, Jennifer Schuster, et al. "Correcting Misperceptions about Cognitive Processing Therapy to Treat Moral Injury: A Response to Gray and Colleagues (This Issue)." *Cognitive and Behavioral Practice* 24 (2017): 388–92.

Ward, Jesmyn. *Sing, Unburied, Sing.* New York: Scribner, 2017.

Weinraub, Bernard. "Reagan Joins Kohl in Brief Memorial at Bitburg Graves." *New York Times.* 6 May 1985. Web.

——. "Wiesel Confronts Reagan on Trip; President to Visit Bergen-Belsen; Survivor of Holocaust Urges Him Not to Stop at German Cemetery." *New York Times.* 20 April 1985. Web.

Wisco, Blair E., et al. "Moral Injury in U.S. Combat Veterans: Results from the National Heath and Resilience in Veterans Study." *Depression and Anxiety* 34.4 (2017): 340–47.

Wood, David. "'I'm a Good Person and Yet I've Done Bad Things': A Warrior's Moral Dilemma." *Huffington Post*. 19–21 March 2014. Web. 22 December 2015.

——. *What Have We Done: The Moral Injury of Our Longest Wars*. New York: Little, Brown, 2016.

Young, Matt. *Eat the Apple*. New York: Bloomsbury, 2018.

Index

Wood, David
    on age of soldiers, 15, 28n15
    on categorizing moral injury, 9, 44
    on defense for moral injury, 10
    on guilt and shame, 13
    on moral injury from wars in
        Afghanistan and Iraq, 127, 130–31
    on moral injury symptoms, 27n14, 40
    on therapies for PTSD, 29

Wordsworth, William, *Prelude*,
    28n16
world, bad feelings about, 40–41
wounds, holding on to, 163–64

Yellow Birds, The (Powers), 134–36,
    140–41, 142, 143, 144, 145–46,
    147–49, 151
Yeomans, Peter, 54, 128

9 781501 755873